LESS TRAVELED LEADERSHIP

ESSENTIAL LEADERSHIP SKILLS

FOR

TODAY'S WORKPLACE

"Learning to Lead for Commitment Rather than Manage for Compliance"

I0532788

Emory Cooper

eBook ISBN: 979-8-89496-516-1

Paperback ISBN: 979-8-89496-517-8

Hardback ISBN: 979-8-89496-513-0

PUBLISHED BY: Broadway Publishing Company

DISCLAIMER AND/OR LEGAL NOTICES

PRINTED IN THE UNITED STATES OF AMERICA

Emory's Leadership style exemplifies corporate values. Often called "The Professor," leaders at all levels call upon him for advice, coaching, and guidance from simple to complex, from a Department Supervisor to the President of the Division. His door is always open, and you can always count on sound advice, even if it's not the popular or easy path to take.

What sets Emory apart as a leader is his ability to think ahead about the impact of decisions, learn something from every situation, and put solutions into practice, ensuring we prevent new issues and strengthen company leadership.

...The Power of One Award

Bulk Book Order

MOTIVATE AND INSPIRE OTHERS!

"Share This Book"

Special Quantity Discounts

5-20 Books	$21.95
21-99 Books	$18.95
100-499 Books	$15.95
500-999 Books	$12.95
1,000+ Books	$9.95

To Place an Order, Contact:

270-528-3083

BroadwayPublishingco.com

Unlock Your Leadership Potential!

Are you inspired by the leadership insights in our latest book? Take the next step in your leadership journey by subscribing to the Broadway Publishing Company's Leadership Newsletter!

Join a community of motivated leaders who receive exclusive content in their inboxes. Our newsletter offers:

- **Expert Articles**: Dive deeper into leadership strategies and real-world applications.
- **Interviews**: Gain wisdom from top industry leaders and influencers.
- **Tips & Tools**: Practical advice and resources to enhance your leadership skills.
- **Event Updates**: Be the first to know about webinars, workshops, and networking opportunities.

Don't miss the chance to grow and refine your leadership abilities continually. Subscribe today and stay ahead with the latest trends, insights, and opportunities designed to empower you as a leader.

Sign up now and start your journey to becoming the leader you aspire to be!

Subscribe at: www.broadwaypublishing.com/leadership-newsletter

DEDICATION

To my incredible children, Bethany, Blake, and Brandon, and to my wonderful grandsons, Isaac, Ian, Elijah, Rhett, and Reed: Your love and support inspire me daily.

To my son-in-law Brooke and my daughter-in-law Monica, I'm glad you are a part of this family. May this book serve as a testament to the strength, wisdom, and joy that family brings.

To My wife, Dale, you keep us all together. Thank you for this!

TABLE OF CONTENTS

PREFACE

The workplace landscape is undergoing significant transformation in a rapidly evolving world. Traditional hierarchical leadership models are being redefined, and the demands on leaders are becoming more complex and multifaceted. Today's leaders must navigate a dynamic environment characterized by technological advancements, cultural shifts, and an unprecedented pace of change. The skills required to lead effectively in this new era are markedly different from those of the past, necessitating a fresh perspective on leadership.

"Less Traveled Leadership: Essential Leadership Skills for Today's Workplace" is a comprehensive guide designed to equip current and aspiring leaders with the tools and insights essential to excel in modern organizational settings. This book explores a range of competencies crucial for effective leadership, from emotional intelligence and communication to strategic thinking and innovation. It recognizes that leadership is not a one-size-fits-all endeavor but a nuanced and adaptive practice that requires a deep understanding of oneself and others.

This book's inspiration stems from my experiences and observations over the years. As a business leader, consultant, and educator, I have witnessed firsthand the challenges leaders face and the qualities that set successful leaders apart. This book's stories and lessons are drawn from diverse industries and backgrounds, providing a rich tapestry of perspectives highlighting effective leadership's universal principles.

This book is structured to provide both theoretical frameworks and practical applications. Each chapter delves into a specific skill or attribute, offering actionable strategies and real-world examples to illustrate key concepts. Whether you are a seasoned executive looking to refine your approach or a new manager aiming to build a solid foundation, you will find valuable insights that can be applied immediately to enhance your leadership capabilities.

In writing this book, I aim to foster a deeper understanding of what it means to lead in today's workplace. I want to inspire leaders at all levels to embrace the challenges and opportunities that come with their roles and to cultivate environments where individuals and teams can thrive. Leadership is a continuous learning and growth journey, and I hope this book will serve as a trusted companion.

Thank you for embarking on this exploration of leadership with me. Together, we can build a future where leaders are effective but also empathetic, innovative, and resilient.

Warm regards,

Emory Cooper

INTRODUCTION

Leadership is critical in any workplace, as it significantly influences an organization's dynamics, culture, and productivity. Effective leadership drives an organization's success by inspiring and guiding employees to achieve common goals. To comprehend leadership in the workplace, it's essential to explore various dimensions, including leadership styles, traits, theories, and the impact of leadership on organizational outcomes.

Investing in leadership development is crucial for sustaining organizational growth and adaptability. Leadership training programs, mentoring, and continuous feedback mechanisms help nurture potential leaders and enhance the skills of existing ones.

Understanding leadership in the workplace involves recognizing the diverse styles, traits, and theories that define effective leadership. The impact of good leadership on employee satisfaction, productivity, and organizational success underscores the importance of cultivating strong leaders within an organization. By fostering a culture of leadership development, organizations can ensure sustained growth and adaptability in an ever-evolving business landscape.

Over the past decade, several key changes have characterized the evolution of employees in the workforce. These changes are influenced by technological advancements, shifting societal norms, and evolving business practices. Here are some of the major transformations:

1. **Technological Savvy and Digital Skills:**

   - **Increased Digital Literacy**: Employees today are more adept at using technology. Familiarity with digital tools, software, and platforms has become essential, driven by the rise of remote work and digital communication.

- **Emphasis on Continuous Learning**: The rapid pace of technological change has necessitated continuous learning. Employees are increasingly engaged in upskilling and reskilling to stay relevant in their fields.

2. **Remote and Flexible Work:**

- **Remote Work Acceptance**: The COVID-19 pandemic accelerated the acceptance and implementation of remote work. Employees now expect greater flexibility in where and how they work. Remote work creates other workplace issues when teamwork and cohesiveness are so important. Some employees changed jobs when companies required the employees to return to reporting to "the office" after the pandemic.

- **Work-Life Balance**: There is a stronger focus on achieving work-life balance, with employees valuing flexible hours and the ability to work from different locations.

3. **Diversity and Inclusion:**

- **Greater Emphasis on Diversity**: A significant push has been made towards creating more diverse and inclusive workplaces. Employees are more aware of and advocate for diversity regarding gender, race, ethnicity, and other aspects.

- **Inclusive Policies**: Companies are implementing policies and practices to ensure an inclusive environment, recognizing the importance of diverse perspectives in driving innovation and performance.

4. **Values and Purpose-Driven Work:**

   - **Alignment with Values**: Employees increasingly seek to work for companies whose values align. They prioritize organizations that are socially responsible and engaged in sustainable practices.

   - **Purpose over Paycheck**: There is a noticeable shift towards valuing meaningful work over merely financial compensation. Employees want to feel that their work has a positive impact on society.

5. **Mental Health and Well-Being:**

   - **Focus on Mental Health**: Awareness around mental health has grown significantly. Employers must support employees' mental well-being through various initiatives and resources.

   - **Holistic Well-Being Programs**: Companies offer more comprehensive well-being programs that address physical, emotional, and mental health.

6. **Gig Economy and Freelance Work:**

   - **Rise of the Gig Economy**: There has been a substantial increase in gig and freelance work. Many employees prefer the flexibility and autonomy of freelance opportunities they can do from home for extra money.

   - **Multiple Income Streams**: Employees are diversifying their income sources, often engaging in projects or entrepreneurial ventures alongside their primary job. My children will be the first to tell you about "the five streams of income" I regularly discussed with them as they became high school and college-aged kids. It is still a part of our conversations when discussing new business adventures.

7. **Collaborative and Flat Structures:**

- **Shift Towards Collaboration**: The traditional hierarchical structure gives way to more collaborative and flat organizational structures. Employees prefer environments where they can collaborate across levels and departments.

- **Empowered Teams**: Teams are more empowered to make decisions, fostering a sense of ownership and accountability among employees.

These changes reflect broader societal and economic trends, indicating a more dynamic, flexible, and values-driven workforce. Employers need to adapt to these shifts to attract and retain talent effectively.

In addition to the workplace changes discussed, the workforce has changed significantly in that several generations are represented, each bringing unique perspectives, values, and working styles. The primary generations include:

1. **Traditionalists (Silent Generation, born before 1946)**

2. **Baby Boomers (born 1946-1964)**

3. **Generation X (born 1965-1980)**

4. **Millennials (Generation Y, born 1981-1996)**

5. **Generation Z (born 1997-2012)**

Characteristics and Leadership Approaches for Each Generation

1. Traditionalists

Characteristics:

- Value hard work, loyalty, and respect for authority.
- Prefer formal communication and a hierarchical structure.
- Less tech-savvy compared to younger generations.

Leadership Approach:

- Respect and Recognition: Show respect for their experience and contributions and publicly acknowledge their hard work and loyalty.
- Structured Environment: Maintain a formal, organized workplace structure.
- Personal Interaction: Use face-to-face meetings and written communication over digital modes of communication.

2. Baby Boomers

Characteristics:

- Ambitious, driven by professional achievements, and value stability.
- Experienced in traditional work environments with hierarchical structures.
- Somewhat adaptable to technology but may prefer traditional communication methods.

Leadership Approach:

- Professional Development: Offer opportunities for career growth and skill development.

- Recognition and Rewards: Implement recognition programs highlighting their achievements and contributions.
- Inclusion in Decision-Making: Engage them in strategic decisions to leverage their experience.

3. Generation X

Characteristics:

- Independent, resourceful, and adaptable.
- Value work-life balance and flexibility.
- Comfortable with technology and informal communication.

Leadership Approach:

- Flexibility: Provide options for flexible work hours and remote work.
- Autonomy: Allow autonomy in their roles and avoid micromanagement.
- Direct Communication: Use straightforward and transparent communication.

4. Millennials

Characteristics:

- Tech-savvy, value collaboration, and continuous feedback.
- Seek meaningful work and a sense of purpose.
- Prefer flat organizational structures and open communication.

Leadership Approach:

- Purpose and Meaning: Connect their work to a larger purpose or mission.

- Collaborative Environment: Foster a team-oriented culture and provide collaborative tools.
- Continuous Feedback: Implement regular feedback mechanisms and mentorship programs.

5. Generation Z

Characteristics:

- Digital natives, highly tech-savvy, and value diversity and inclusion.
- Seek stability and job security despite a preference for entrepreneurial ventures.
- Desire immediate feedback and rapid career progression.

Leadership Approach:

- Technology Integration: Utilize advanced digital tools and platforms for communication and collaboration.
- Diversity and Inclusion: Promote an inclusive workplace culture with diverse teams.
- Career Development: Provide clear career paths, mentorship, and opportunities for rapid advancement.

To facilitate leadership for a multigeneration workforce, here are some general rules to make it easier to meet the expectations of each team member:

General Leadership Strategies for a Multigenerational Workforce

1. Tailored Communication: Adjust communication styles to meet each generation's preferences, from formal to informal and face-to-face to digital.

2. Flexibility and Work-Life Balance: Implement flexible working arrangements, such as remote work and flexible hours, to cater to the varying needs of different generations.

3. Continuous Learning: Offer continuous learning and development opportunities to keep all generations engaged and updated with the latest skills and technologies.

4. Mentorship Programs: Create mentorship programs where experienced employees can share their knowledge with younger generations, fostering mutual learning.

5. Inclusive Culture: Promote an inclusive culture that values diversity in age, experience, and background, ensuring all employees feel respected and valued.

By understanding and addressing each generation's unique needs and preferences, leaders can create a harmonious and productive workplace where all employees thrive. It might be a good idea to periodically check the team's expectations and adjust the strategies accordingly.

Importance of Leadership in The Workplace

You may be wondering why so much importance is being placed on leadership in the workplace today. The environment of the business world and the employees in the workplace demand that businesses and leaders up their game to stay competitive in the market and bring the best employees into their organization.

Leadership plays a critical role in shaping the success of an organization. Effective leadership provides a **vision and direction** for the organization and sets the overall direction for many aspects of the company. Leaders articulate goals, values, and objectives, guiding the organization toward a common purpose.

Leaders **inspire and motivate** employees to perform at their best. By providing encouragement, recognition, and support, leaders foster a positive work environment where employees feel engaged and committed to achieving organizational goals.

Leaders **make key decisions** that impact the direction and growth of the organization. Leaders leverage their expertise, experience, and judgment to ensure that decisions align with the organization's mission and values and contribute to its success.

Leaders shape the organizational **culture and core values** such as integrity, transparency, and accountability. They establish norms and behaviors that guide how employees interact with one another and with external stakeholders.

Effective leadership prioritizes talent development within the organization. Leaders identify and nurture high-potential employees, provide opportunities for growth and advancement, and foster a culture of continuous learning and development.

In a rapidly changing business environment, leadership drives innovation and fosters **adaptability**. Leaders encourage creativity and risk-taking, empowering employees to embrace change and seize new opportunities.

Leaders facilitate **communication and collaboration** across all levels of the organization. Leaders create a cohesive and aligned workforce capable of tackling complex challenges by fostering open dialogue, sharing information transparently, and encouraging teamwork.

Leaders manage **stakeholder relations** with customers, investors, suppliers, and the community. Leaders enhance the organization's reputation and long-term sustainability by building trust, cultivating partnerships, and demonstrating a commitment to stakeholder interests.

Leaders are responsible for **performance management**. They establish performance standards and hold employees accountable for results. By identifying specific performance deficiencies and providing feedback, coaching, and recognition, leaders drive continuous improvement and ensure that the organization achieves its objectives effectively and efficiently.

Strong leadership is essential during times of crisis or uncertainty to guide the organization through **challenges and adversity**. Leaders demonstrate resilience, adaptability, and decisiveness, instilling confidence and stability across the organization amid uncertainty.

Effective **leadership is a fundamental driver of organizational success.** It influences every aspect of the business, from strategy and culture to performance and resilience.

Impact of Poor Leadership in The Workplace

With the absence of good leadership in the workplace, poor leadership can appear in many ways within an organization and at many levels, including the department, group, or team. We've identified some good leadership qualities, and you can probably identify the results of poor leadership. If you have been in the workforce for a period, you may have lived through some of them. Check out the list:

1. **Low morale:** When leaders fail to inspire and motivate their team members, morale can quickly fall to an all-time low. A byproduct of this fall is that employees may become disengaged, leading to lower productivity and higher turnover levels.

2. **High turnover:** Employees are more likely to leave an organization with poor leadership. In fact, many employee surveys identify their manager as the primary reason why they leave a company.

3. **Resistance to change:** A strong leadership culture may be needed to navigate a company through harsh market conditions. Employees may be reluctant to change

unless the employees view the reason for change as reasonable.

4. **Communication breakdown:** Effective communication is essential for any organization to operate smoothly. If leaders throughout the organization fail to communicate with their individual teams, this leads to misunderstanding, conflicts, and decreased interaction among the various teams or departments.

5. **Loss of trust**: Trust is essential for effective leadership. Trust erodes when leaders are perceived as incompetent, dishonest, or self-serving, making it difficult to rally employees around common goals and initiatives.

6. **Negative organizational culture:** Poor leadership can create a toxic work environment characterized by politics, favoritism, and fear. Such a culture cannot retain top talent, and such a reputation will soon inform the community why people may not want to work for this organization.

7. **Micromanagement:** Insecure or incompetent leaders may resort to micromanaging their employees, which can be demoralizing and stifling. It undermines trust and autonomy, leading to reduced innovation and creativity.

8. **Lack of accountability and finger-pointing:** Poor leaders may fail to hold themselves and others accountable for their actions and performance. This lack of accountability can foster a culture of mediocrity and undermine the organization's success.

9. **Poor Decision-Making:** Leaders who lack the necessary skills or experience may make poor decisions that negatively impact the organization or team, resulting

in wasted resources, missed opportunities, and damaged reputation.

10. **Lack of Direction:** Poor leadership often results in a lack of clear vision and direction for the organization or team. Without a strong leader who clearly sets goals and priorities, employees may feel confused about what they should work towards.

Writing a book on leadership skills for today's workplace is valuable and timely for several compelling reasons:

1. Evolving Workplace Dynamics

The modern workplace is rapidly changing due to technological advancements, remote work, and shifting cultural expectations. Leadership in this context requires new skills and approaches to manage virtual teams, foster collaboration across digital platforms, and maintain productivity without the traditional office environment.

2. Increasing Importance of Soft Skills

There is a growing recognition of soft skills such as emotional intelligence, communication, empathy, and adaptability. Influential leaders today must master these skills to navigate the complexities of diverse and inclusive work environments, which are crucial for fostering a positive workplace culture and driving organizational success.

3. High Demand for Leadership Development

Organizations across industries invest heavily in leadership development to prepare employees for future roles. A book on leadership skills can provide a structured and comprehensive resource for current and aspiring leaders to develop these essential competencies, offering practical advice and strategies based on contemporary challenges and opportunities.

4. Addressing Leadership Gaps

Many organizations need more qualified leaders to meet their needs. A book on leadership skills can contribute to closing this gap by providing insights, frameworks, and tools that help individuals transition into leadership roles more effectively and confidently.

5. Enhancing Employee Engagement and Retention

Effective leadership is a crucial driver of employee engagement and retention. Leaders who are well-equipped with the right skills can create an environment where employees feel valued, motivated, and supported, which is critical for retaining top talent and reducing turnover rates.

6. Responding to Generational Shifts

As new generations enter the workforce, their expectations and values differ from those of previous generations. Leaders must understand and adapt to these changes to effectively manage and inspire a multigenerational workforce. A book focused on leadership skills can provide insights into managing these dynamics and leveraging the strengths of a diverse team.

7. Navigating Crisis and Change

The past few years have underscored the importance of solid leadership in times of crisis and change. Whether dealing with a global pandemic, economic uncertainty, or rapid technological disruption, leaders need specific skills to guide their organizations through turbulent times. A leadership book can guide resilience, crisis management, and strategic thinking.

8. Promoting Innovation and Creativity

Innovation and creativity are critical for success in today's competitive business environment. Influential leaders need to cultivate these qualities within their teams. A book on leadership skills can provide strategies for fostering an innovative culture, encouraging creative problem-solving, and maintaining a competitive edge.

9. Building Ethical and Sustainable Practices

Modern leadership increasingly emphasizes ethical behavior and sustainability. Leaders are expected to uphold high ethical standards and make decisions that benefit their organizations, society, and the environment. A leadership skills book can address these topics, guiding leaders on integrating ethical considerations and sustainability into their decision-making processes.

10. Personal Growth and Fulfillment

Finally, developing leadership skills contributes to personal growth and fulfillment. For many individuals, effective leadership is not just about professional success but also about achieving personal goals, building meaningful relationships, and positively impacting others.

In conclusion, writing a book on leadership skills for today's workplace addresses critical needs and offers valuable guidance for navigating the complexities of modern leadership. It can be a powerful tool for personal and professional development, ultimately contributing to the success and well-being of individuals and organizations. I have witnessed the successes and failures of some people in a leadership role, and their ability to navigate the workplace determines their fate. Some didn't have a clue of what they were doing or were too cocky to admit they needed to learn more about leadership.

Types of Leadership Styles

In today's workplace, various leadership styles are often observed, each with its characteristics and approaches. Here are some common ones:

Transactional Leadership: This style focuses on exchanges between leaders and followers, where rewards or punishments are given based on performance. It's more about maintaining the status quo and completing tasks efficiently. Transactional Leadership is a style of management that focuses on supervision, organization, and performance; it is based on a system of rewards and punishments. This leadership style often contrasts with transformational Leadership, which seeks to inspire and motivate employees beyond immediate tasks.

Critical Characteristics of Transactional Leadership

1. **Clear Structure**: Transactional leaders establish clear, structured roles and responsibilities. They ensure that expectations are well-defined and that team members understand their tasks.

2. **Rewards and Punishments**: This leadership style relies heavily on rewards and punishments to motivate employees. Rewards are given for meeting or exceeding expectations, while punishments are used for failing to meet standards.

3. **Short-term Goals**: Transactional Leadership focuses on short-term goals and immediate results. Leaders in this style prioritize efficiency and adherence to established procedures.

4. **Management by Exception**: Transactional leaders often practice management by exception, which involves

monitoring performance and intervening only when standards are not met. There are two types of management by exception:

- **Active**: The leader monitors the work and corrects issues as they arise.

- **Passive**: The leader intervenes only after a problem has become severe.

5. **Directive Leadership**: Transactional leaders provide specific instructions and closely supervise tasks. Their directive approach ensures compliance with rules and policies.

Advantages of Transactional Leadership

1. **Clarity and Consistency**: Provides clear expectations and consistent feedback, which can help improve performance and productivity.

2. **Efficiency**: Focuses on established procedures and rules, which can streamline processes and increase efficiency.

3. **Motivation through Rewards**: Rewards can motivate employees to perform well and achieve specific goals.

4. **Performance Monitoring**: Continuous monitoring helps quickly identify and correct deviations from standards.

Disadvantages of Transactional Leadership

1. **Limited Creativity**: This style can stifle creativity and innovation since it emphasizes adherence to rules and procedures over new ideas.

2. **Employee Dependency**: Employees can depend on the leader for direction, reducing their autonomy and initiative.

3. **Short-term Focus**: Emphasis on immediate results may overlook long-term growth and development.

4. **Potential for Demotivation**: Over-reliance on punishments can lead to a hostile work environment, reducing morale and engagement.

Applications of Transactional Leadership

Transactional Leadership is often effective in situations where tasks are routine and clearly defined, such as:

- **Military**: Where strict adherence to orders and regulations is crucial.

- **Manufacturing and Production**: Where efficiency and precision are essential.

- **Sales**: Where specific targets and performance metrics can drive results.

Conclusion

Transactional Leadership is a practical and effective approach for managing teams where clear structure and immediate results are necessary. However, its limitations suggest that it is best complemented with other leadership styles that foster creativity, long-term growth, and employee development.

Transformational Leadership: Transformational leaders inspire and motivate their team members by emphasizing vision, innovation, and personal development. They often lead by example and encourage creativity and collaboration. Transformational Leadership is a style of Leadership where leaders inspire and motivate their followers to achieve their full potential and exceed their expectations. This type of Leadership fosters growth, change, and innovation. Here are the key components and characteristics of transformational Leadership:

1. **Inspirational Motivation**: Transformational leaders have a clear vision for their followers. They are enthusiastic and optimistic, which helps to inspire and motivate their team to work towards common goals.

2. **Intellectual Stimulation**: These leaders encourage creativity and innovation. They challenge their followers to think critically and solve problems in new and different ways, which involves questioning assumptions, reframing issues, and approaching old situations with new methodologies.

3. **Individualized Consideration**: Transformational leaders pay attention to the individual needs of their followers. They act as mentors or coaches and provide personalized support and encouragement to help each team member grow and develop, which involves recognizing and addressing individual strengths and weaknesses.

4. **Idealized Influence**: Transformational leaders serve as role models for their followers. They are admired, respected, and trusted. These leaders demonstrate high standards of ethical conduct and make personal sacrifices for the group's benefit, setting a powerful example for others to follow.

Benefits of Transformational Leadership

- **Enhanced Performance and Productivity**: Transformational leaders can significantly enhance team performance and productivity by inspiring and motivating followers. Followers often exceed their expectations and achieve higher levels of performance.

- **Increased Innovation**: Encouraging creativity and intellectual stimulation leads to higher levels of innovation within the organization. Followers are more likely to devise novel solutions to problems and drive the organization forward.

- **Improved Morale and Job Satisfaction**: Transformational Leadership can lead to higher job satisfaction and morale among followers. Employees who feel valued and supported are more engaged and committed to their work.

- **Personal and Professional Growth**: The focus on individualized consideration helps followers to develop their skills and abilities, leading to personal and professional growth. This not only benefits the individual but also contributes to the overall success of the organization.

Examples of Transformational Leaders

- **Steve Jobs**, the co-founder of Apple Inc., was known for his visionary leadership skills and ability to inspire and motivate his team to achieve extraordinary innovation and excellence.

- **Nelson Mandela**: As a transformational leader, Mandela inspired a nation with his vision of equality and his commitment to justice and reconciliation.

- **Jeff Bezos**: The founder of Amazon, Bezos is known for his innovative thinking and his ability to inspire his team to push the boundaries of what is possible in e-commerce and technology.

Developing Transformational Leadership

To develop transformational leadership qualities, individuals can focus on the following:

- **Cultivate a Clear Vision**: Develop a compelling vision to guide and inspire your followers.

- **Foster a Culture of Innovation**: Encourage creativity and innovation by challenging assumptions and promoting new ways of thinking.

- **Support and Develop Followers**: Provide individualized support and mentorship to help your team members grow and achieve their full potential.

- **Lead by Example**: Demonstrate high standards of ethical behavior and lead by example to earn the trust and respect of your followers.

Transformational Leadership can drive significant positive change in organizations by harnessing its members' collective energy and creativity. Transformational leaders can build high-performing teams that can achieve remarkable outcomes through inspiration, intellectual stimulation, individualized consideration, and idealized influence.

Servant Leadership: Servant leaders prioritize the needs of their team members above their own. They focus on empowering others, fostering a supportive environment, and enabling individual growth and success.

Servant Leadership is a philosophy in which the leaders' main goal is to serve. This style is different from traditional Leadership, where the leaders' primary focus is the thriving of their company or organization. A servant leader shares power, puts the needs of others first, and helps people develop and perform as highly as possible.

Critical Concepts of Servant Leadership

1. **Serving First**: A servant leader prioritizes the needs of employees and the community. They focus on providing support and resources to help others succeed.

2. **Empathy**: Servant leaders strive to understand and empathize with others. They care deeply about the well-being of their team members.

3. **Healing**: Servant leaders seek to heal and improve their team's emotional health. They recognize and address issues that hinder personal and professional growth.

4. **Awareness**: It is crucial to be aware of oneself and others. This involves understanding personal strengths and weaknesses and recognizing the impact of one's actions on others.

5. **Persuasion**: Rather than relying on authority, servant leaders use persuasion and influence to encourage people to follow.

6. **Conceptualization**: Servant leaders think beyond day-to-day realities to envision the future. They balance short-term goals with long-term objectives.

7. **Foresight**: This involves predicting outcomes and understanding the lessons from the past to make better decisions.

8. **Stewardship**: They take responsibility for their entrusted roles and act as caretakers for the organization and its people.

9. **Commitment to People's Growth**: A servant leader is committed to the personal and professional growth of everyone in the organization.

10. **Building Community**: They work to create a sense of belonging and cohesion within the organization.

Benefits of Servant Leadership

- **Employee Satisfaction and Engagement**: Servant leadership increases employee satisfaction and engagement, as employees feel valued and supported.

- **Trust and Cooperation**: By prioritizing the needs of others, servant leaders build strong trust and cooperation within teams.

- **Personal Development**: Team members are more likely to develop and improve their skills under a servant leader committed to their growth.

- **Organizational Success**: Organizations with servant leaders often see better performance and success because employees are motivated and aligned with the leader's vision.

Challenges of Servant Leadership

- **Time-Consuming**: Implementing servant leadership can be time-consuming, as it requires a significant investment in people and their development.

- **Perceived Weakness**: Some may perceive Servant Leadership as a sign of weakness or lack of authority.

- **Balance**: Servant leaders must balance serving others and making tough decisions that benefit the organization.

Conclusion

Servant Leadership is a powerful approach that can transform organizations by prioritizing employee well-being and development. It fosters a positive and productive work environment, leading to long-term success and growth. However, it requires a genuine commitment to serving others and to balance various organizational needs.

Democratic Leadership: This style involves participative decision-making, where leaders seek input and consensus from team members before making decisions. It promotes inclusivity, creativity, and a sense of ownership among employees.

Democratic Leadership, or participative Leadership, is a leadership style where leaders actively involve team members in decision-making. This style emphasizes collaboration, open communication, and sharing responsibility and authority. Here are some key features and benefits of democratic Leadership:

Key Features

1. **Participation and Involvement:**

   - Leaders seek input and feedback from team members before making decisions.

   - Team members are encouraged to share ideas and suggestions.

2. **Shared Decision-Making:**

   - Decisions are made collectively, often through discussions and voting.

   - The leader acts as a facilitator, guiding the process rather than dictating outcomes.

3. **Open Communication:**

   - There is a high level of transparency in communication.

   - Information flows freely between leaders and team members.

4. **Empowerment:**
   - Team members have the autonomy to take initiative and make decisions within their areas of responsibility.
   - Leaders trust their teams and delegate tasks appropriately.

5. **Collaboration:**
   - Teamwork and cooperation are highly valued.
   - The leader fosters a collaborative environment where everyone works towards common goals.

Benefits of Democratic Leadership

1. **Increased Engagement:**
   - Team members feel valued and respected, leading to higher motivation and job satisfaction.
   - Engaged employees are more committed and productive.

2. **Better Decision-Making:**
   - The inclusion of diverse perspectives leads to more comprehensive and well-rounded decisions.
   - It reduces the risk of errors and biases a single leader might have.

3. **Development of Team Members:**
   - Participation in decision-making helps team members develop their skills and confidence.
   - It prepares them for future leadership roles.

4. **Enhanced Innovation:**
   - Encouraging ideas from all team members fosters creativity and innovation.
   - The team is more likely to develop unique solutions to problems.

5. **Strong Team Cohesion:**
   - Collaborative efforts build trust and strengthen relationships among team members.
   - A cohesive team is more resilient and adaptable to change.

Challenges

1. **Time-Consuming:**
   - The process of seeking input and reaching a consensus can be time-consuming.
   - It may slow down decision-making in fast-paced environments.

2. **Conflict Management:**
   - Differences in opinions can lead to conflicts.
   - The leader needs strong conflict resolution skills to manage disagreements effectively.

3. **Dependence on Team Competence:**
   - The effectiveness of democratic Leadership depends on the competence and willingness of team members to participate.
   - Inexperienced or uninterested members can hinder the process.

4. **Potential for Indecision:**

- Reaching a consensus can sometimes take time, leading to indecision or delayed actions.
- The leader must balance participation with the need to make timely decisions.

Application

Democratic Leadership is particularly effective in environments that value creativity, innovation, and employee development. It is seen in:

- **Creative industries such as** advertising, design, and media companies where innovation and new ideas are crucial.
- **In education,** where collaborative teaching and learning methods are emphasized.
- **Non-profits and NGOs:** Organizations that rely on the active involvement of volunteers and staff to fulfill their missions.

Democratic Leadership promotes a collaborative and inclusive work environment that can improve employee satisfaction, decision-making, and innovation. However, it requires skilled leaders who can effectively manage the process and address the challenges associated with this style.

Autocratic Leadership: Autocratic leaders make decisions independently without seeking input from others. They tend to have strict control over their team and enforce rules and procedures strictly, which can lead to efficiency but may also stifle innovation and morale.

Autocratic Leadership, also known as authoritarian Leadership, is a management style characterized by individual control over all decisions with little input from group members. Autocratic leaders typically make choices based on their ideas and judgments and rarely accept advice from followers. Here are the key features and implications of autocratic Leadership:

Key Features

1. **Centralized Decision-Making**: The leader makes decisions independently with little or no input from others.

2. **Strict Control and Regulation**: Leaders closely supervise and regulate the activities of their subordinates.

3. **Clear Expectations and Rules**: The leader provides clear expectations and specific guidance on what needs to be done.

4. **Limited Group Participation**: Followers have minimal influence on decisions and limited participation in the leadership process.

5. **Fast Decision-Making**: Decisions are made quickly since often only one person is responsible for the outcome.

Advantages

1. **Efficiency**: Decisions are made rapidly without group deliberation.

2. **Clear Direction**: Provides clear directives and expectations, reducing ambiguity.

3. **Control**: Effective in crises where decisive action is needed.

4. **Productivity**: This can lead to high productivity when the leader is knowledgeable and experienced.

Disadvantages

1. **Low Morale**: Subordinates may feel undervalued and discontented due to lack of input.

2. **Dependency**: Over-reliance on the leader for decisions can stifle initiative and creativity among subordinates.

3. **High Turnover**: This can lead to high employee turnover due to dissatisfaction and lack of empowerment.

4. **Resistance**: Resistance and lack of cooperation from team members may be encountered.

5. **Limited Innovation**: Suppression of team input can hinder innovative ideas and solutions.

Situations Suited for Autocratic Leadership

- **Military**: Often used in military settings where strict control and quick decision-making are crucial.

- **Crisis Management**: Useful in emergencies where immediate decisions are necessary.

- **Inexperienced Teams**: Can be effective with teams that require close supervision and guidance.

Notable Autocratic Leaders

- **Steve Jobs (Apple)** was known for his meticulous and controlling management style, which led to innovative products but also created a demanding work environment.

- **Henry Ford (Ford Motor Company)** implemented strict processes and control in manufacturing, leading to the efficient production of automobiles.

Conclusion

While Autocratic Leadership can be effective in certain situations, especially where quick decision-making is critical, it often leads to lower employee satisfaction and morale. Balancing autocratic practices with participative elements can mitigate drawbacks, fostering a more inclusive and motivated work environment.

Laissez-Faire Leadership: In this hands-off approach, leaders provide minimal guidance and allow team members to make most decisions independently. It can promote autonomy and creativity but may need more direction and accountability if appropriately managed.

Laissez-faire Leadership is a management style characterized by a hands-off approach. Leaders provide minimal direction and allow team members to make decisions and solve problems. This type of Leadership relies heavily on team members' competence and initiative, granting them the autonomy to manage their tasks and responsibilities independently.

Key Characteristics of Laissez-Faire Leadership:

1. **Minimal Supervision**:
   - Leaders offer little guidance or supervision, trusting team members to manage their own work.
   - Decision-making authority is decentralized, and employees have significant freedom in approaching tasks.

2. **Autonomy and Independence**:
   - Team members are encouraged to take initiative and make decisions without needing approval from higher-ups.
   - Creativity and innovation are often fostered, as employees can explore different methods and solutions.

3. **Responsibility and Accountability**:
   - Employees are held accountable for their own performance and outcomes.
   - Successes and failures rest primarily on the individual's abilities and efforts.

4. **Trust in Team Members**:

- Leaders have a high level of trust in their team members' skills and judgment.
- This style is most effective when team members are highly skilled, experienced, and self-motivated.

5. **Limited Interaction**:

- Interaction between leaders and team members is often limited to essential communications.
- Leaders may step in only when necessary, such as in crises or significant issues.

Advantages of Laissez-Faire Leadership:

1. **Encourages Innovation**:

- Freedom and autonomy can lead to creative and innovative solutions, as strict guidelines do not constrain employees.

2. **Empowers Employees**:

- Team members often feel more valued and empowered, increasing job satisfaction and motivation.

3. **Develop skills and Leadership**:

- This style can help develop employees' problem-solving skills and leadership abilities, preparing them for future roles.

4. **Increased Flexibility**:

- Teams can be more adaptable and responsive to changes, as they are used to working independently and making decisions on the fly.

Disadvantages of Laissez-Faire Leadership:

1. **Lack of Direction**:

   - Without clear guidance, teams may struggle with a lack of direction, leading to inefficiencies or confusion.

2. **Potential for Low Productivity**:

   - Employees who are not self-motivated may take advantage of the lack of oversight, resulting in decreased productivity.

3. **Inconsistency**:

   - The quality of work may vary significantly among team members, leading to inconsistencies in performance and outcomes.

4. **Inadequate Problem Solving**:

   - Teams might face difficulties when complex problems arise, especially if they lack the experience or knowledge to address them without guidance.

When Laissez-Faire Leadership Works Best:

- **Highly Skilled and Experienced Teams**:

  - This style is most effective with teams that are knowledgeable and capable of working independently.

- **Creative Industries**:

  - Fields that benefit from innovation and creative problem-solving, such as tech startups, research and development, and creative industries, can thrive under laissez-faire leadership.

- **Motivated and Self-Driven Individuals**:
    - Employees who are naturally motivated, responsible, and enjoy autonomy are well-suited to this leadership style.

In summary, laissez-faire leadership can be highly effective in environments where employees are skilled, motivated, and capable of working independently. However, it requires a careful balance to ensure that the lack of direct supervision does not lead to issues with productivity or direction.

Coach-style Leadership: Leaders using this style focus on developing the skills and capabilities of their team members. They provide guidance, feedback, and support to help individuals reach their full potential.

Coach-style Leadership is a leadership approach that emphasizes guiding and developing team members to achieve their full potential. This style is akin to how sports coaches work with athletes, focusing on individual strengths, fostering skill development, and encouraging continuous improvement. Here are some key characteristics and benefits of coach-style Leadership:

Characteristics of Coach Style Leadership

1. **Personal Development Focus**:
    - Leaders prioritize the growth and development of their team members, both professionally and personally. They work to identify everyone's strengths and areas for improvement.

2. **Active Listening and Empathy**:
    - Coaches are attentive listeners who show empathy. They seek to understand their team members' perspectives and provide support tailored to their needs.

3. **Constructive Feedback**:

   - Feedback is provided regularly and is constructive. It focuses on helping individuals understand what they are doing well and where they can improve, often with specific, actionable advice.

4. **Goal Setting**:

   - Leaders work with team members to set clear, achievable goals. These goals often align with both organizational objectives and personal aspirations.

5. **Mentorship and Guidance**:

   - Instead of simply directing, coach-style leaders mentor and guide their team members, helping them navigate challenges and learn from experiences.

6. **Empowerment and Autonomy**:

   - Team members are empowered to take initiative and make decisions. Leaders trust their teams and encourage independence while providing the necessary support.

7. **Emphasis on Learning**:

   - Continuous learning is encouraged. Leaders often promote a culture where people see mistakes as opportunities for learning rather than as failures.

Benefits of Coach Style Leadership

1. **Improved Performance**:
   - By focusing on individual development, team members often perform better as they are more skilled and motivated.

2. **Higher Engagement and Motivation**:
   - Employees feel valued and understood, which boosts their engagement and motivation. They are more likely to be committed to their work and the organization.

3. **Increased Innovation**:
   - Empowered employees are more likely to take initiative and think creatively, leading to more innovative solutions and ideas.

4. **Stronger Team Relationships**:
   - The emphasis on empathy and support strengthens relationships within the team, fostering a collaborative and supportive environment.

5. **Retention of Talent**:
   - Employees are more likely to stay with an organization where they feel supported and see opportunities for growth and development.

Implementing Coach Style Leadership

To implement Coach-Style Leadership effectively, leaders can take the following steps:

1. **Develop Active Listening Skills**:
   - Practice active listening techniques, such as maintaining eye contact, nodding, and summarizing the other person's words to ensure understanding.

2. **Provide Regular Feedback**:
   - Schedule regular feedback sessions and ensure that feedback is specific, balanced, and growth-focused.

3. **Set SMART Goals**:
   - Work with team members to set Specific, Measurable, Achievable, Relevant, and Time-bound goals.

4. **Encourage Self-Reflection**:
   - Promote a culture where team members regularly reflect on their performance and identify areas for improvement.

5. **Facilitate Learning Opportunities**:
   - Provide access to training, workshops, and other learning resources. Encourage team members to pursue professional development.

6. **Model Coaching Behavior**:
   - Lead by example. In your interactions with others, demonstrate coaching behaviors that emphasize the importance of support and development.

Coach-style Leadership can transform teams and organizations by fostering a culture of continuous improvement, collaboration, and mutual support. By focusing on individual development and empowerment, this leadership style can lead to sustainable success and a more fulfilling work environment.

These are just a few examples, and many leaders incorporate elements of multiple styles depending on the situation and the needs of their team. Effective Leadership often involves flexibility and adaptability to various circumstances and personalities within the workplace.

Understanding the Difference Between a Supervisor/Manager and a Leader

In the contemporary business environment, people often discuss the roles of supervisors, managers, and leaders, sometimes interchangeably; however, while overlapping in certain aspects, these roles hold distinct characteristics that significantly differentiate them. Understanding these differences is crucial for the effective functioning of organizations, as each role contributes uniquely to the overall success. This essay delves into the fundamental distinctions between supervisors or managers and leaders, highlighting their core functions, approaches, and impacts on organizational dynamics.

The Role of Supervisors and Managers

Supervisors and managers play a pivotal role in an organization's operational functionality. Their primary responsibilities revolve around ensuring that tasks are completed efficiently and effectively. This includes overseeing employees' work, implementing policies, and maintaining order within the workplace.

Core Responsibilities

1. **Task Management:** Supervisors and managers focus on the day-to-day operations. They are responsible for planning, organizing, and controlling work processes to meet organizational goals. This involves assigning tasks, setting deadlines, and monitoring progress.

2. **Resource Allocation:** Supervisors and managers must effectively utilize resources. They ensure the necessary human, financial, or material resources are available and used efficiently to achieve the set objectives.

3. **Policy Implementation:** Supervisors and managers implement and enforce organizational policies. They ensure that employees adhere to company rules and regulations, which helps maintain a structured and disciplined work environment.

4. **Performance Monitoring:** Monitoring and evaluating employee performance is integral to supervisors' and managers' roles. This involves conducting performance reviews, providing feedback, and taking corrective actions when necessary.

Approach and Style

Supervisors and managers typically adopt a more authoritative and directive approach. Their focus is on maintaining control and ensuring compliance with established procedures. This often involves a top-down communication style where directives are issued from higher management and cascaded down to subordinates.

1. **Directive Approach:** Supervisors and managers often give explicit instructions and expect them to be followed. This approach ensures clarity and reduces ambiguity in task execution.

2. **Control and Compliance:** Emphasis is placed on control mechanisms to ensure that employees adhere to organizational standards. Managers and supervisors enforce compliance through regular monitoring and corrective actions.

The Role of Leaders

Leadership, on the other hand, transcends the traditional functions of management. Leaders are visionaries who inspire and motivate employees to achieve organizational goals and personal and professional growth. Their influence extends beyond task completion to fostering a culture of innovation and engagement.

Core Responsibilities

1. **Vision and Strategy:** Leaders define the organization's vision and strategic direction. They articulate a compelling vision that inspires and aligns employees' efforts toward common objectives.

2. **Inspiration and Motivation:** Leaders motivate and inspire their teams. They create an environment where employees feel valued, empowered, and driven to contribute their best efforts.

3. **Change Management:** Leaders are crucial in managing change within organizations. They guide their teams through transitions, helping them adapt to new processes, technologies, and market conditions.

4. **Development and Mentorship:** Leaders invest in their team members' personal and professional development. They act as mentors and coaches, providing guidance and support to help employees realize their potential.

Approach and Style

Leaders adopt a more transformational and participative approach. They focus on building relationships, fostering collaboration, and encouraging innovation. Their communication style is often more open and inclusive, promoting dialogue and feedback.

1. **Transformational Approach:** Leaders inspire change and innovation. They challenge the status quo and encourage their teams to think creatively and explore new possibilities.

2. **Participative Style:** Leaders involve their team members in decision-making processes. They value employee input and foster a sense of ownership and accountability.

Key Differences

The distinctions between supervisors/managers and leaders can be understood through several key dimensions:

1. **Focus on Tasks vs. Focus on People:** Supervisors and managers are primarily task-oriented, focusing on task execution and achieving immediate goals. Leaders, however, are people-oriented, emphasizing their teams' development, motivation, and engagement.

2. **Authority vs. Influence:** Supervisors and managers rely on their positional authority to direct and control employees. On the other hand, leaders rely on their ability to influence and inspire, gaining voluntary commitment from their team members.

3. **Short-term vs. Long-term Perspective:** Supervisors and managers often operate with a short-term focus, concentrating on immediate tasks and objectives. Leaders adopt a long-term perspective, envisioning the future and setting strategic goals.

4. **Directive vs. Inspirational:** Supervisors and managers communicate more directly, providing clear instructions and expectations. Leaders communicate inspirationally, motivating employees to exceed expectations and pursue excellence.

Interplay Between Management and Leadership

While the distinctions between supervisors/managers and leaders are clear, it is essential to recognize that effective organizational performance often requires a blend of both. Supervisors and managers must incorporate leadership qualities to inspire and engage their teams, while leaders need to understand and manage operational details to ensure that their vision is implemented effectively.

1. **Integrating Leadership into Management:** Managers can enhance their effectiveness by adopting leadership behaviors such as active listening, empathy, and motivational communication. This helps in building a more engaged and committed workforce.

2. **Operationalizing Vision:** Leaders must translate their vision into actionable plans and processes. Understanding management principles enables leaders to implement their strategies effectively, ensuring that organizational goals are met.

In conclusion, while supervisors/managers and leaders serve distinct roles within an organization, both are essential for success. Supervisors and managers ensure operational efficiency and policy adherence, while leaders inspire and motivate teams toward a shared vision. The most effective organizations recognize the value of both roles and foster a culture where management and leadership coexist and complement each other. Understanding and appreciating the differences between these roles enables organizations to harness the strengths of both, leading to sustained success and growth.

The Five Functions of Management

Management is a crucial aspect of any organization, determining its ability to achieve objectives, adapt to changing environments, and grow sustainably. Henri Fayol, a pioneer in the field of management theory, identified five primary functions of management that are essential for the successful operation of any organization: Planning, Organizing, Leading, Controlling, and Coordinating. Let's explore these functions, their significance, interconnections, and practical applications in contemporary management practices.

1. Planning

Definition and Importance

Planning is the foundational function of management. It involves formulating detailed steps to achieve organizational goals. It is a forward-looking process that directs all other management functions. Effective planning helps organizations anticipate challenges, allocate resources efficiently, and align activities with strategic objectives.

Types of Planning

There are various types of planning, including strategic, tactical, operational, and contingency planning.

- **Strategic Planning:** Long-term and broad, focusing on the organization's direction.

- **Tactical Planning:** Shorter-term, more specific plans that outline implementing strategic plans.

- **Operational Planning:** Day-to-day plans that ensure the organization's smooth operation.

- **Contingency Planning:** Plans for unexpected events or emergencies, ensuring the organization can respond swiftly to crises.

Steps in the Planning Process

1. **Setting Objectives:** Define clear, measurable goals.

2. **Analyzing Situations:** Assess internal and external environments using tools like SWOT analysis.

3. **Developing Plans:** Formulate strategies and actions to achieve the objectives.

4. **Implementing Plans:** Put the strategies into action.

5. **Monitoring and Reviewing:** Continuously assess progress and make necessary adjustments.

Real-world Application

Planning is more dynamic in the contemporary business environment due to rapid technological advancements and global market changes. Companies like Apple Inc. exemplify effective planning by continuously innovating and adapting their strategies to stay ahead in the competitive tech industry.

2. Organizing

Definition and Importance

Organizing is the process of structuring resources and activities to achieve objectives efficiently. It involves creating a framework for the division, coordination, and control of tasks and the flow of information within the organization.

Key Elements of Organizing

- **Work Specialization:** Dividing tasks into specific jobs.

- **Departmentalization:** Grouping jobs into departments based on function, product, geography, or customer.

- **Chain of Command:** Establishing clear lines of authority and responsibility.

- **Span of Control:** Determining the number of employees a manager can effectively supervise.

- **Centralization vs. Decentralization:** Deciding how much decision-making is concentrated at upper levels or dispersed throughout the organization.

Steps in the Organizing Process

1. **Identifying Activities:** Determine all the tasks that must be performed.

2. **Grouping Activities:** Combine similar tasks into manageable units.

3. **Assigning Duties:** Allocate tasks to individuals or teams.

4. **Delegating Authority:** Grant the necessary authority to perform tasks.

5. **Establishing Relationships:** Define lines of communication and reporting.

Real-world Application

Google's organizational structure, known for its flexibility and innovation, highlights the importance of effective organizing. Google fosters creativity and rapid problem-solving by promoting a culture of collaboration and empowering employees through decentralization.

3. Leading

Definition and Importance

Leading involves motivating, influencing, and guiding employees toward achieving organizational goals. It is a dynamic and interpersonal function of management that focuses on managing people rather than tasks.

Key Aspects of Leading

- **Motivation:** Encouraging employees to perform at their best.

- **Communication:** Ensuring clear and compelling exchange of information.

- **Leadership Styles:** Adapting different styles (e.g., autocratic, democratic, laissez-faire) based on the situation and team needs.

- **Team Building:** Fostering a sense of unity and cooperation among team members.

Leadership Theories

- **Trait Theory** focuses on identifying the innate qualities and characteristics of leaders.

- **Behavioral Theory** emphasizes the behavior and actions of leaders rather than their traits.

- **Contingency Theory** suggests that the effectiveness of a leadership style depends on the context.

- **Transformational Leadership** is when the leaders inspire and motivate employees to exceed their own self-interest for the organization's good.

Real-world Application

A prime example of effective leadership is Satya Nadella's tenure as CEO of Microsoft. By fostering a growth mindset and encouraging innovation, Nadella revitalized Microsoft and led it to new heights in the tech industry.

4. Controlling

Definition and Importance

Controlling is the function of management that involves monitoring performance, comparing it with objectives, and implementing necessary corrective actions. It ensures that organizational activities are aligned with established plans and standards.

Steps in the Controlling Process

1. **Setting Performance Standards:** Establish clear and measurable standards.

2. **Measuring Actual Performance:** Collect data on performance metrics.

3. **Comparing Performance with Standards:** Identify deviations from the set standards.

4. **Taking Corrective Actions:** Implement measures to address any discrepancies.

Types of Control

- **Feedforward Control:** Anticipating problems before they occur.

- **Concurrent Control:** Monitoring ongoing activities to ensure they conform to standards.

- **Feedback Control:** Evaluating results after activities are completed.

Tools for Control

- **Budgets:** Financial plans that outline expected revenues and expenditures.

- **Audits:** Systematic examination of records and processes.

- **Performance Appraisals:** Regular assessment of employee performance.
- **Balanced Scorecard:** A strategic planning and management tool that views the organization from multiple perspectives.

Real-world Application

Toyota's use of Total Quality Management (TQM) exemplifies the controlling function. Toyota maintains high product quality and operational efficiency standards by implementing rigorous quality control measures and continuous improvement practices.

5. Coordinating

Definition and Importance

Coordinating is the management function that ensures different departments and teams work together harmoniously to achieve common objectives. It involves aligning activities, resolving conflicts, and facilitating cooperation among diverse organizational units.

Key Aspects of Coordinating

- **Synchronization:** Ensuring all parts of the organization move in harmony.
- **Communication:** Facilitating the flow of information between departments.
- **Conflict Resolution:** Addressing and managing conflicts to prevent disruption.
- **Resource Allocation:** Ensuring resources are distributed effectively to where they are needed most.

Steps in the Coordinating Process

1. **Understanding Objectives:** Ensure all departments understand the organizational goals.

2. **Establishing Clear Roles:** Define the roles and responsibilities of each team.

3. **Fostering Communication:** Create channels for effective communication.

4. **Monitoring Progress:** Regularly check the alignment of activities with objectives.

Real-world Application

Effective coordination is critical in the healthcare industry. In hospitals, coordinating the activities of doctors, nurses, administrative staff, and various departments ensures efficient patient care and operational effectiveness.

The five functions of management—Planning, Organizing, Leading, Controlling, and Coordinating—are interrelated and essential for the success of any organization. These functions provide a comprehensive framework for managers to guide their teams, make informed decisions, and achieve organizational goals. Understanding and implementing these functions effectively can improve efficiency, productivity, and adaptability in a rapidly changing business environment. As management practices evolve, these fundamental functions remain relevant, offering timeless principles for achieving excellence in organizational performance.

Personal Leadership Assessment Gauge

It's Free! Do it!

Congratulations on your progress in reading this book! Let's dive deeper!

Enhance your leadership journey with a Personal Assessment Gauge. Identify your current thoughts on your strengths and areas you would like to improve upon to champion your Leadership style in the workplace.

Request your Gauge today

www.broadwaypublishingco.com/leadershipassessment/

PART ONE:
PERSONAL LEADERSHIP SKILLS

Throughout my career, I have been an employee in several organizations, consulted with 52 companies on organization development and associate relations, focused on employment law compliance, and rarely did I hear any discussions about the concept of leadership. Additionally, I taught Supervision courses at the college level. I quickly became aware that what I had to teach in these courses would have been unknown to many people functioning as supervisors and other leaders in the business world. It all came down to the level of leadership in the organization.

Self-Awareness and Emotional Intelligence

Self-awareness for a leader in the workplace involves a deep understanding of one's strengths, weaknesses, values, emotions, and motivations and how these factors impact their behavior and interactions with others. It means recognizing and acknowledging personal biases, limitations, and blind spots.

For a leader, self-awareness is crucial because it allows them to:

1. **Understand their Impact:** Self-aware Leaders can recognize how their words, actions, and decisions affect those around them, including their team members and colleagues.

2. **Adapt and Grow:** Self-aware leaders can consciously improve their skills and behaviors by understanding their strengths and weaknesses and seeking development opportunities and feedback to grow continuously.

3. **Build Authentic Relationships:** Self-aware leaders are more authentic and genuine in their interactions, which fosters trust and respect among team members. They can communicate openly, listen actively, and empathize with others' perspectives.

4. **Make Better Decisions:** Being self-aware helps leaders make more informed and rational decisions because they can consider

their biases and emotions. They are also more open to considering diverse viewpoints and alternatives.

5.   **Manage Stress and Emotions:** Leaders face various challenges and pressures in the workplace, and self-awareness helps them manage stress effectively and regulate their emotions. They can recognize when they are becoming overwhelmed and take steps to address it constructively.

Self-awareness is a cornerstone of effective leadership. It enables leaders to lead with authenticity, empathy, and integrity while fostering a positive and productive work environment.

Emotional intelligence (EI) is paramount for leaders in the workplace as it directly influences their ability to navigate complex interpersonal dynamics, inspire teams, and drive organizational success. Here are some critical aspects of emotional intelligence for leaders:

1.   **Self-awareness:** Effective leaders are in tune with their emotions, strengths, weaknesses, and values. They understand how their moods and actions impact others and are open to feedback for self-improvement.

2.   **Self-regulation:** Leaders with high EI can manage their emotions, impulses, and reactions, even in challenging situations. They remain composed under pressure, think before acting, and adapt to changing circumstances without becoming overwhelmed.

3.   **Empathy:** Empathetic leaders demonstrate genuine concern for the feelings and perspectives of others. They listen attentively, seek to understand different viewpoints, and cultivate a culture of inclusivity and collaboration.

4.   **Social skills:** Leaders skilled in social interactions can build and maintain positive relationships with colleagues, clients, and stakeholders. They communicate effectively, resolve conflicts diplomatically, and inspire team trust and loyalty.

5.   **Motivation:** Leaders with intrinsic solid motivation set ambitious goals, persevere in the face of setbacks, and inspire others with passion and optimism. They foster a sense of purpose and enthusiasm that drives individual and collective performance.

6.   **Emotional resilience:** In a fast-paced and often stressful work environment, emotionally intelligent leaders demonstrate resilience in bouncing back from setbacks, failures, or criticism. They view challenges as opportunities for growth and encourage their teams to do the same.

7.   **Cultural sensitivity:** In today's globalized workplace, leaders must be culturally aware and sensitive to their team members' diverse backgrounds, beliefs, and values. They recognize the importance of inclusivity and strive to create an environment where everyone feels valued and respected.

By honing these emotional intelligence skills, leaders can cultivate stronger relationships, foster a positive work culture, and drive sustainable organizational success.

Managing emotions effectively is crucial for leaders in the workplace to maintain productivity, foster positive relationships, and navigate challenges successfully. Here are some strategies for managing emotions in leadership:

1. **Recognize and acknowledge emotions:** Leaders should be aware of their own emotions as well as the emotions of others. Recognizing emotions allows leaders to respond appropriately and make informed decisions.

2. **Pause and reflect:** When faced with a challenging situation or strong emotions, leaders must take a moment to pause and reflect before reacting. This allows them to respond thoughtfully rather than impulsively.

3. **Practice active listening:** Empathetically listening to employees' concerns and perspectives can help leaders

understand the underlying emotions driving their behavior, which can foster trust and strengthen relationships within the team.

4. **Communicate effectively:** Clear and open communication is vital to managing emotions in the workplace. Leaders should express themselves honestly and respectfully while encouraging open dialogue among team members.

5. **Set boundaries:** Leaders must establish boundaries to maintain their emotional well-being and prevent burnout. Setting boundaries may involve delegating tasks, saying no when necessary, and prioritizing self-care.

6. **Lead by example:** Leaders who model emotional intelligence and self-regulation set a positive example for their team members. By demonstrating calmness under pressure and handling conflicts constructively, leaders inspire others to do the same.

7. **Seek support:** Leaders need a support system, whether it's mentoring, coaching, or peer networks. Having someone to talk to can provide perspective and help leaders manage their emotions effectively.

8. **Practice empathy:** Empathy allows leaders to understand and connect deeply with their team members. Leaders can respond to emotions with compassion and support by putting themselves in others' shoes.

9. **Manage stress:** Leaders must proactively manage stress to prevent it from negatively impacting their emotions and decision-making. This may involve practicing mindfulness, exercising regularly, and maintaining a healthy work-life balance.

10. **Seek feedback:** Leaders should be open to receiving feedback from their team members about how they handle

emotions in the workplace. Constructive feedback can help leaders identify areas for improvement and continue developing their emotional intelligence skills.

By implementing these strategies, leaders can effectively manage their emotions in the workplace, foster a positive work environment, and support the well-being and success of their team members. Self-awareness is a crucial aspect of personal growth and development. Here's a structured exercise to help you enhance your self-awareness:

Self-Awareness Exercise

Step 1: Reflect on Your Values

Purpose: Understand what is most important to you.

1. **List Your Core Values:** Write down 5-10 values most important to you (e.g., honesty, family, success, creativity, compassion).

2. **Prioritize Your Values:** Rank these values in order of importance to you.

3. **Reflect on Each Value:** For each value, write a few sentences about why it is important to you and how it influences your actions and decisions.

Step 2: Identify Your Strengths and Weaknesses

Purpose: Gain insight into your abilities and areas for improvement.

1. **Strengths:** List your top 5 strengths. Consider skills, talents, and positive traits.

2. **Weaknesses:** List your top 5 weaknesses. Consider areas where you struggle or need improvement.

3. **Reflect:** For each strength and weakness, write a few sentences about how they manifest in your life and impact you.

Step 3: Analyze Your Emotional Responses

Purpose: Understand your emotional triggers and responses.

1. **Identify Triggers:** Think of recent situations that triggered strong emotional responses (both positive and negative). Write down these situations.

2. **Analyze Reactions:** For each situation, describe your emotional reaction. What did you feel? How did you react?

3. **Understand the Cause:** Reflect on why these situations triggered these responses. What underlying beliefs or past experiences might be influencing your emotions?

Step 4: Set Personal Goals

Purpose: Define what you want to achieve and create a plan to get there.

1. **Short-Term Goals:** Write down 3-5 short-term goals (to be achieved within the next year).

2. **Long-Term Goals:** Write down 3-5 long-term goals (to be achieved within the next 5-10 years).

3. **Action Plan:** Outline the steps you need to take to achieve each goal. Be specific and include deadlines if possible.

Step 5: Seek Feedback

Purpose: Gain external perspectives to enhance self-awareness.

1. **Choose Trusted Individuals:** Identify 3-5 people whose opinions you trust and who know you well (e.g., friends, family, colleagues).

2. **Ask for Feedback:** Request feedback on your strengths and weaknesses and how you can improve. Be open and receptive to their input.

3. **Reflect on Feedback:** Compare their feedback with your self-assessment. What are the similarities and differences? How can you use this feedback for personal growth?

Step 6: Practice Mindfulness

Purpose: Develop present-moment awareness and improve emotional regulation.

1. **Mindful Breathing:** Practice mindful breathing for 5-10 minutes daily. Focus on your breath and let go of any distracting thoughts.

2. **Daily Reflection:** At the end of each day, take a few minutes to reflect on your experiences. What did you learn about yourself today?

3. **Mindful Activities:** Incorporate mindfulness into daily activities (e.g., eating, walking, or working). Pay full attention to the present moment.

Keeping a Journal

Document your reflections and insights in a journal to be able to track your progress and deepen your self-awareness over time.

Engaging regularly in this exercise can help you develop a deeper understanding of yourself, improve your emotional intelligence, and guide your personal and professional growth.

Emotional Intelligence Exercise: The Daily Reflection

Objective: Enhance your emotional intelligence by reflecting on daily experiences and identifying emotions, triggers, and responses.

Step 1: Daily Journal

1. **End of Day Reflection:**
   - Spend 10-15 minutes at the end of each day reflecting on your experiences.

- Write down three significant events that happened during the day. These can be positive, negative, or neutral.

2. **Identify Emotions:**

   - For each event, note the emotions you felt. Be specific (e.g., happy, frustrated, anxious, excited, etc.).

3. **Recognize Triggers:**

   - Identify what triggered these emotions. Was it something someone said? An unexpected event? What are your thoughts or actions?

4. **Analyze Responses:**

   - Reflect on how you responded to these emotions. Did you react impulsively? Did you take a moment to process your feelings? How did your response affect the situation?

Step 2: Empathy Practice

1. **Put Yourself in Others' Shoes:**

   - For one event each day, try to understand other people's emotions.

   - Write down what you think they might have felt and why.

2. **Empathetic Communication:**

   - Think about how you could have communicated more empathetically. Could you have listened more actively, shown more understanding, or responded differently?

Step 3: Emotional Regulation Techniques

1. **Breathing Exercises:**

   - Practice deep breathing exercises when you identify strong emotions during the day. Take a few deep breaths to calm yourself before responding.

2. **Positive Self-Talk:**

   - Develop a habit of positive self-talk. When you notice negative emotions, counter them with positive affirmations or realistic reassessments.

3. **Mindfulness Meditation:**

   - Spend 5-10 minutes each day practicing mindfulness meditation. Focus on being present and observing your thoughts and feelings without judgment.

Step 4: Weekly Review

1. **Weekly Summary:**

   - At the end of the week, review your daily entries.
   - Identify any patterns or recurring triggers and responses.

2. **Set Goals:**

   - Set small, achievable goals for the next week based on your reflections. For example, "I will practice active listening in meetings" or "I will use deep breathing to manage stress."

Step 5: Share and Discuss

1. **Find a Partner:**

   - Share your experiences and reflections with a trusted friend, family member, or mentor. Discussing your insights can provide new perspectives and enhance your understanding.

2. **Seek Feedback:**

- Ask for feedback on how you handle your emotions and interactions. Use this feedback to improve your emotional intelligence further.

By consistently practicing these steps, you'll develop a deeper understanding of your emotions, enhance your empathy, and improve your ability to regulate your emotional responses.

Goal Setting and Time Management

Goal setting and time management go hand in hand, forming the cornerstone of personal and professional development. Here's a breakdown to help you effectively manage both:

Goal Setting:

Specificity: Define your goals clearly. Vague goals are more challenging to achieve.

Measurableity: Establish criteria to track your progress. Quantify your goals whenever possible.

Achievability: Set realistic goals that challenge you but are within your reach.

Relevance: Ensure your goals align with your values, priorities, and long-term objectives.

Time-boundedness: Set deadlines for your goals to add a sense of urgency and helps prioritize tasks.

Time Management:

1. **Prioritize**: Identify your most important tasks and tackle them first. Use techniques like the Eisenhower Matrix to prioritize effectively.

2. **Plan**: Break down your goals into smaller tasks and create a schedule. Use tools like calendars, planners, or apps to organize your time.

3. **Eliminate distractions**: Identify distractions and minimize them. This could mean setting boundaries with Technology, creating a dedicated workspace, or managing interruptions.

4. **Delegate**: Learn to delegate tasks others can do, freeing time for more critical activities.

5. **Review and adjust**: Regularly review your goals and progress. Adjust your plans as needed based on changes in circumstances or priorities.

Strategies for Effective Time Management:

1. **Pomodoro Technique**: Work for a set period (e.g., 25 minutes) and then take a short break. Repeat this cycle to maintain focus and productivity.

2. **Time Blocking**: Allocate specific blocks of time for different tasks or activities. This helps prevent multitasking and ensures you dedicate focused time to each task.

3. **Batching**: Group and tackle similar tasks together in one go. For example, respond to emails or phones during designated time slots rather than sporadically throughout the day.

4. **Limit Multitasking**: Focus on one task at a time to improve efficiency and reduce errors.

5. **Technology Wisely**: Leverage productivity tools and apps to streamline tasks, manage schedules, and stay organized.

Combining practical goal setting with efficient time management techniques can enhance productivity, help you achieve your objectives, and lead a more fulfilling life.

Setting SMART Goals

SMART" is an acronym commonly used in goal setting to make objectives more effective. Each letter stands for a critical component of a well-defined goal:

1.   Specific: Goals should be clear and specific, answering the questions of who, what, where, when, and why. Being specific helps in understanding exactly what is expected.

2.   Measurable: Goals should be quantifiable, allowing progress to be tracked and measured. It's important to establish concrete criteria for measuring progress toward the attainment of each goal.

3.   **Achievable**: Goals should be realistic and attainable within the available resources and timeframe. While it's good to set ambitious goals, they should still be within reach with effort and commitment.

4.   **Relevant**: Goals should align with broader objectives and be relevant to the individual or organization setting them. They should contribute to overall success and be meaningful in the context in which they are set.

5.   **Time-bound**: Goals should have a defined timeframe or deadline for completion. This helps create a sense of urgency and provides a clear target to work towards.

The SMART criteria can help ensure that goals are well-defined, feasible, and actionable, increasing the likelihood of success.

Prioritizing Tasks Effectively

Prioritizing tasks effectively is crucial for maximizing productivity and achieving goals efficiently. Here are some strategies to help you prioritize effectively:

1.   **Set Clear Goals**: Understand your short-term and long-term objectives. Align your tasks with these goals to ensure you're working on what truly matters.

2. **Urgent vs. Important**: Use the Eisenhower Matrix or similar frameworks to differentiate between urgent and important tasks. First, focus on urgent and essential tasks, followed by important but not urgent ones.

3. **Deadline Awareness**: Prioritize tasks with approaching deadlines. This will help you manage your time effectively and ensure you don't miss any critical deadlines.

4. **Use of Priority Levels**: Assign priority levels to tasks based on their importance and urgency. This can be done using high, medium, or low-priority labels.

5. **Consider Impact**: Evaluate the potential impact of completing each task. Focus on tasks that will have the most significant impact on your goals or projects.

6. **Break Down Tasks**: Break down larger tasks into smaller, more manageable sub-tasks. This makes prioritizing and tackling tasks one step at a time more manageable.

7. **Time Blocking**: Allocate specific time blocks for different tasks or categories. This helps you focus on one task at a time and prevents distractions.

8. **Consider Resources**: Consider the resources (time, money, manpower, etc.) required to complete each task. Prioritize tasks that align with your available resources.

9. **Personal Energy Levels**: Be aware of your peak energy times during the day and schedule important or challenging tasks during these periods.

10. **Regular Reviews**: Review your task list regularly to update priorities based on changes in deadlines, goals, or circumstances.

11. **Learn to Delegate**: Identify tasks that can be delegated to others, especially if they are not the best use of your time or skills.

12. **Flexibility**: Be flexible and willing to adapt your priorities. Unexpected events or changes may require you to adjust your task list accordingly.

By incorporating these strategies into your daily routine, you can prioritize tasks effectively and stay focused on what truly matters, ultimately increasing your productivity and achieving your goals more efficiently.

Overcoming Procrastination

Procrastination can be challenging, but many people struggle with it. Here are some strategies to help you overcome procrastination:

1. **Break tasks into smaller steps**: Sometimes, tasks can seem overwhelming, leading to procrastination. Break them down into smaller, more manageable steps. This can make them feel less daunting and more accessible to start.

2. **Set specific goals and deadlines**: Set clear, achievable goals for yourself and establish deadlines to complete them. A deadline can create a sense of urgency and motivate you to start.

3. **Use a timer**: Set a timer for a short period of time, like 25 minutes, and work on a task without any distractions during that time. This technique, known as the Pomodoro Technique, can help you focus and progress on your tasks.

5. **Eliminate distractions**: Identify and eliminate any distractions that might tempt you to procrastinate. This could include turning off your phone, closing unnecessary tabs on your computer, or finding a quiet workplace.

6. **Find your optimal working environment**: Some people work best in a quiet environment, while others prefer background noise. Experiment with different environments to find what works best for you.

7. **Reward yourself**: Create a system of rewards for yourself for completing tasks or reaching milestones. This will help motivate you to stay on track and avoid procrastination.

8. **Practice self-compassion**: Be kind to yourself if you procrastinate occasionally. Instead of dwelling on past procrastination, focus on what you can do to move forward.

9. **Identify and address the root cause**: Sometimes, procrastination can be a symptom of underlying issues like fear of failure, perfectionism, or lack of interest. Try to identify what's causing you to procrastinate and address it directly.

10. **Use positive reinforcement**: Instead of focusing on the negative consequences of procrastination, focus on the positive benefits of completing tasks on time. Visualize how good it will feel to accomplish your goals.

11. **Seek support**: Share your goals with friends, family, or colleagues who can help keep you accountable and provide support and encouragement.

Remember, overcoming procrastination is a process, and it's okay to have setbacks along the way. The important thing is to keep trying and find strategies that work best for you.

Goal Setting Exercise

Goal setting is a powerful exercise to help you clarify your objectives and create a plan to achieve them. Here's a step-by-step guide to setting practical goals:

Step 1: Define Your Vision

- **Visualize Your Future**: Imagine where you want to be in the next 1, 5, or 10 years. Consider all aspects of your life: career, personal development, health, relationships, and hobbies.

- **Write It Down**: Clearly describe your vision in paragraphs or bullet points.

Step 2: Set Specific Goals

- **SMART Criteria**: Ensure your goals are Specific, Measurable, Achievable, Relevant, and Time-bound.
  - **Specific**: Clearly define what you want to accomplish.
  - **Measurable**: Identify how you will measure progress and determine when you have achieved the goal.
  - **Achievable**: Set goals that are challenging but attainable.
  - **Relevant**: Ensure the goals align with your vision and values.
  - **Time-bound**: Set a deadline for achieving the goal.

Step 3: Break Down Your Goals

- **Milestones**: Divide each goal into smaller, manageable tasks or milestones.
- **Action Plan**: Create a detailed plan outlining the steps needed to reach each milestone.

Step 4: Identify Resources and Obstacles

- **Resources**: List the tools, skills, and support you need to achieve your goals.
- **Obstacles**: Identify potential challenges and brainstorm solutions to overcome them.

Step 5: Take Action

- **Start Small**: Begin with the first task or milestone. Taking small, consistent steps will build momentum.

- **Monitor Progress**: Regularly review and adjust your plan as needed.

Step 6: Stay Motivated

- **Celebrate Successes**: Reward yourself for achieving milestones.

- **Stay Positive**: Keep a positive mindset and remind yourself of your vision.

- **Seek Support**: Share your goals with a friend, mentor, or coach for encouragement and accountability.

Step 7: Review and Reflect

- **Regular Check-ins**: Schedule regular times to review your progress and make any necessary adjustments.

- **Reflect on Learnings**: Consider what works well and can be improved.

TIME MANAGEMENT EXERCISE

Time management is a crucial skill. Let's start by identifying your needs and goals. Here are some steps and questions to guide you:

Step 1: Identify Your Goals

1. What are your short-term and long-term goals?
2. What tasks or activities are most important for achieving these goals?

Step 2: Assess Your Current Time Management

1. How do you currently spend your time?
2. What activities take up most of your time?
3. Are there any timewasters or distractions you want to minimize?

Step 3: Prioritize Your Tasks

1. Which tasks are most urgent and vital?
2. Which tasks can be delegated or postponed?

Step 4: Plan Your Schedule

1. What is your ideal daily or weekly schedule?
2. How can you allocate time for high-priority tasks?
3. What tools or methods can help you stay organized (e.g., to-do lists, calendars, apps)?

Step 5: Implement and Adjust

1. How will you implement your new schedule?
2. How will you monitor and adjust your plan to improve your time management?

Practical Exercise

Let's put this into a practical exercise. Please answer the following questions to get started:

1. List three short-term goals (within the next month) and three long-term goals (within the next year).
2. Describe a typical day in your current schedule.
3. Identify three significant timewasters or distractions in your current routine.
4. List five tasks you need to complete this week and rank them in order of importance.

We can create a tailored time management plan for you by answering these questions.

Example of Goal Setting

Vision

"I want to be a successful author who writes engaging and inspiring fiction. I want to live a balanced life with strong relationships and good health."

Goals

1. **Write and Publish a Novel (1 Year)**
   - **Specific**: Write a 70,000-word fiction novel.
   - **Measurable**: Complete 5,000 words each month.
   - **Achievable**: Allocate 1 hour daily for writing.
   - **Relevant**: Aligns with my vision of being a successful author.
   - **Time-bound**: Complete the manuscript in 12 months.

2. **Improve Physical Health (6 Months)**
   - **Specific**: Lose 10 pounds and run a 5k.
   - **Measurable**: Track weight loss and running distance weekly.
   - **Achievable**: Follow a balanced diet and exercise plan.
   - **Relevant**: Supports my goal of living a balanced life.
   - **Time-bound**: Achieve within six months.

3. **Action Plan for Writing and Publishing a Novel**
   - **Month 1**: Outline the plot and characters.
   - **Months 2-7**: Write 10,000 words per month.
   - **Month 8**: First draft complete, take a break.

- **Months 9-10**: Revise and edit.
- **Month 11**: Seek feedback from beta readers.
- **Month 12**: Final revisions and submission to publishers.

Resources Needed

- Writing software (e.g., Scrivener)
- Books on writing techniques
- Support from a writing group or mentor.

Potential Obstacles and Solutions

- **Obstacle**: Writer's block

    o **Solution**: Take breaks, read for inspiration, and set a routine.

- **Obstacle**: Lack of time

    o **Solution**: Prioritize writing and schedule dedicated time daily.

Following this structured approach, you can set clear, actionable goals and create a roadmap to achieve your vision.

Decision Making and Problem Solving

Decision-making and problem-solving are crucial skills for leaders in the workplace. Here are some key strategies for effective decision-making and problem-solving:

1. **Define the Problem**: Identify your issue or challenge. This involves understanding the root cause and its impact on the organization.

2. **Gather Information**: Collect relevant data and information to understand the problem and its context better. This might involve conducting research, gathering stakeholder input, or analyzing past experiences.

3. **Generate Alternatives**: Brainstorm multiple potential solutions or courses of action. Encourage creativity and diverse perspectives during this stage.

4. **Evaluate Alternatives**: Assess the pros and cons of each alternative based on criteria such as feasibility, cost, impact, and alignment with organizational goals and values.

5. **Make the Decision**: Based on your evaluation, select the best alternative. Consider the potential risks and benefits associated with each option.

6. **Implement the Decision**: Develop a plan to implement the decision. Communicate the decision to relevant stakeholders and allocate resources as needed.

7. **Monitor and Evaluate**: Continuously monitor the implementation of the decision and evaluate its effectiveness. If necessary, adjust the course based on feedback and changing circumstances.

8. **Learn and Adapt**: Reflect on the decision-making process and outcomes to identify lessons learned. Use this knowledge to improve future decision-making and problem-solving efforts.

In addition to these steps, influential leaders demonstrate essential qualities such as decisiveness, critical thinking, emotional intelligence, and the ability to collaborate and communicate effectively. They understand that decision-making and problem-solving are often iterative processes that require flexibility and adaptability.

Decision-Making Frameworks

A decision-making framework is a structured approach to making choices or solving problems. It helps individuals or organizations navigate complex situations by providing a systematic process to evaluate options and reach a conclusion. Here's a simple decision-making framework you can use:

1.   **Identify the decision:** Clearly define the problem or decision you must make. If necessary, break it down into smaller, manageable components.

2.   **Gather information:** Collect all relevant information and data related to the decision. This may involve researching, consulting experts, or analyzing past experiences.

3.   **Identify alternatives:** Brainstorm and list all possible options or solutions to the problem. Be creative and consider various perspectives.

4.   **Evaluate alternatives:** Assess each alternative based on predetermined criteria such as feasibility, cost, time, impact, and alignment with goals or values. Consider the potential risks and benefits associated with each option.

5.   **Decide:** Select the best alternative based on the evaluation. Trust your judgment, but also consider input from others if applicable.

6.   **Implement the decision:** Develop a plan for the chosen alternative. Assign responsibilities, allocate resources, and set deadlines as needed.

7.   **Monitor and review:** Continuously assess the decision's outcomes. Monitor progress, gather feedback, and adjust if necessary. Learn from both successes and failures to improve future decision-making processes.

Remember that decision-making is often iterative, and revisiting and revising your choices based on new information or changing circumstances is okay. Flexibility and adaptability are critical components of effective decision-making frameworks.

Decision-Making Exercise

Step 1: Define the Problem

Clearly articulate the problem or decision that needs to be made. Ensure that you understand the context and the implications of the decision.

Example Problem: Choosing the best city to relocate to for a new job opportunity.

Step 2: Gather Information

Collect all relevant information that will help you make the decision. This might include facts, data, opinions, and other necessary details.

Information Needed:

- Job opportunities and market trends in each city.
- Cost of living in each city.
- Quality of life indicators (e.g., healthcare, education, entertainment).
- Climate and environment.
- Proximity to family and friends.
- Personal preferences and lifestyle.

Step 3: Identify Alternatives

List all possible alternatives available. In this case, these would be the different cities you are considering.

Alternatives:

1. New York City, NY
2. San Francisco, CA
3. Austin, TX
4. Seattle, WA

5. Denver, CO

Step 4: Weigh the Evidence

Evaluate each alternative against a set of criteria. You can use a decision matrix or a similar tool to compare the options systematically.

Criteria and Weighting:

- Job Opportunities: 30%
- Cost of Living: 25%
- Quality of Life: 20%
- Climate: 10%
- Proximity to Family: 10%
- Personal Preferences: 5%

Create a table and score each city on a scale of 1 to 10 for each criterion, then multiply by the weight to get a weighted score.

Step 5: Choose Among Alternatives

Based on the weighted scores, determine which alternative is the best option.

Step 6: Act

Plan to implement the decision. This might involve applying for jobs, arranging a visit to the city, or starting the relocation process.

Step 7: Review the Decision

After some time, evaluate the outcome of your decision. Did it meet your expectations? What could you have done differently?

Example Decision Matrix

Criteria	Weight	NYC	SF	Austin	Seattle	Denver
Job Opportunities	0.30	9	8	7	8	6
Cost of Living	0.25	3	2	8	6	7
Quality of Life	0.20	7	7	8	8	8
Climate	0.10	6	8	7	5	6
Proximity to Family	0.10	4	3	7	6	5
Personal Preferences	0.05	7	6	8	7	7
Total Score		6.1	5.95	7.45	6.85	6.75

In this example, Austin has the highest score based on the criteria and weighting, making it the best option according to this analysis.

Final Notes

- **Flexibility**: Be prepared to adapt if new information arises.

- **Consultation**: Discuss with trusted friends or mentors.

- **Intuition**: Sometimes, your gut feeling is important too.

Problem-Solving Techniques

Here are a few problem-solving techniques that can be helpful in various situations:

1. **Define the Problem**: Clearly articulate what the issue is. Sometimes, the problem might not be what it initially appears to be, so taking time to understand the root cause is crucial.

2. **Brainstorming**: Gather a group of people, if possible, and generate as many ideas as possible without initial judgment. Quantity often leads to quality in brainstorming sessions.

3. **Break it Down**: Divide the problem into smaller, more manageable parts. This can make it easier to tackle each component individually.

4. **Mind Mapping**: Create a visual representation of the problem and its potential solutions. This can help to organize thoughts and identify relationships between different aspects of the problem.

5. **SWOT Analysis**: Evaluate the problem's strengths, weaknesses, opportunities, and threats. This structured approach can provide a comprehensive understanding of the situation.

6. **Utilize Data and Evidence**: Gather relevant data and evidence to inform your decision-making process. This helps ensure that your solutions are based on facts rather than assumptions.

7. **Consider Alternatives**: Don't settle for the first solution that comes to mind. Explore multiple options and consider the potential consequences of each before deciding.

8. **Seek Feedback**: Get input from others, especially those with experience or expertise. Fresh perspectives can often lead to innovative solutions.

9. **Trial and Error**: Be bold and try different approaches, even if they seem unconventional. Learning from mistakes is an integral part of the problem-solving process.

10. **Continuous Improvement**: Once a solution is implemented, monitor its effectiveness and be willing to adjust as needed. Problem-solving is often an iterative process.

Remember, there's no one-size-fits-all approach to problem-solving, so feel free to adapt these techniques to suit your specific situation.

Handling Decision-Making Challenges

Decision-making can indeed be challenging, but there are strategies to make it easier:

1. **Define the Problem**: Clearly understand what decision needs to be made and what the desired outcome is.

2. **Gather Information**: Collect all relevant information and data related to the decision. This could involve research, consultation, or analysis.

3. **Identify Alternatives**: Brainstorm and list all possible options available. Don't limit yourself initially; include both evident and creative solutions.

4. **Evaluate Alternatives**: Assess each alternative against criteria such as feasibility, potential risks, costs, and benefits. This could involve decision-making tools like decision matrices or pros and cons lists.

5. **Consider Stakeholders**: Consider how the decision will impact the stakeholders—their perspectives and concerns.

6. **Make the Decision**: Choose the best alternative carefully. Trust your judgment and be open to adjusting if new information arises.

7. **Implement the Decision**: Develop an action plan to implement the decision. Communicate the decision and its rationale to relevant parties.

8. **Evaluate the Outcome**: Monitor the decision results to see if it's achieving the desired outcome. Learn from both successes and failures to improve future decision-making.

Remember, not all decisions will have a perfect solution, and it's okay to make mistakes if you learn from them. Trust your instincts, but also be willing to seek advice and input from others when needed.

Management Skills Training

Enhancing Results Through Managing Performance

Join us for an exclusive training program sponsored by Broadway Publishing Co. and presented by Emory Cooper, the author of "Less Traveled Leadership: Essential Leadership Skills for Today's Workplace." This unique event, "Enhancing Results Through Managing Performance," will occur on December 10, 2024, at 2:00 PM EDT.

Effective performance management is crucial for achieving outstanding results in today's competitive business environment. With his extensive experience and deep insights, Emory Cooper will guide you through proven strategies to optimize team performance and drive organizational success.

During this dynamic session, you'll learn how to set clear objectives, provide constructive feedback, and foster a culture of continuous improvement. Emory's practical approach and actionable advice will enhance productivity, motivate your team, help you achieve your business goals, and empower you to do so.

Don't miss this opportunity to elevate your leadership skills and gain valuable insights from one of the industry's top experts. Reserve your spot now and take the first step towards transforming your management approach and boosting your team's performance.

Register today to secure your place in this highly anticipated virtual event. Together, let's unlock your organization's potential and achieve remarkable results!

PART TWO:
INTERPERSONAL LEADERSHIP SKILLS

Practical communication skills are essential for workplace leaders to foster collaboration, inspire their team, and drive success. Here are some essential communication skills every workplace leader should develop:

1. **Active Listening**: Leaders should listen attentively to their team members, demonstrating empathy and understanding. Active listening involves giving full attention to the speaker, asking clarifying questions, and providing feedback to ensure comprehension.

2. **Clarity and Conciseness**: Leaders should communicate their ideas clearly and concisely, avoiding jargon and unnecessary complexity. Clear communication helps prevent misunderstandings and ensures everyone is on the same page.

3. **Empathy**: Understanding and acknowledging the feelings and perspectives of team members fosters trust and strengthens relationships. Leaders should show empathy in their communication and consider the emotions of their team when delivering feedback or addressing issues.

4. **Transparency**: Open and honest communication builds trust within the team. To keep everyone informed and engaged, leaders should openly share relevant information, including goals, challenges, and decisions.

5. **Adaptability**: Effective leaders adapt their communication style to suit different situations and individuals. They recognize that not everyone communicates or receives information in the same way and adjust their approach accordingly.

6. **Feedback Skills**: Providing constructive feedback is crucial for employee growth and development. Leaders should deliver feedback in a timely and respectful manner, focusing on specific behaviors and offering suggestions for improvement.

7. **Conflict Resolution**: Addressing conflicts promptly and constructively is essential for maintaining a positive work environment. Leaders should facilitate open discussions, listen to all parties involved, and work collaboratively to find solutions that satisfy everyone's needs.

8. **Storytelling**: Crafting compelling narratives helps leaders convey their vision, inspire others, and foster a sense of purpose. Storytelling allows leaders to make complex ideas more relatable and memorable, driving engagement and alignment within the team.

9. **Nonverbal Communication**: Body language, facial expressions, and tone of voice can convey as much meaning as words. Leaders should recognize their nonverbal cues to ensure their message is being received as intended.

10. **Respect and Courtesy**: Treating others respectfully and courteously lays the foundation for positive relationships and effective communication. Leaders should show appreciation for their team members' contributions and value their perspectives, even when there are differences of opinion.

By continuously honing these communication skills, workplace leaders can create a supportive and productive environment where team members feel heard, valued, and motivated to achieve their goals.

Effective Listening

Effective listening is crucial for workplace leaders as it fosters trust, enhances communication, and promotes team collaboration. Here are some strategies for workplace leaders to improve their listening skills:

1. **Give Undivided Attention**: When someone is speaking to you, give them your full attention. Avoid distractions like phones or computers, and maintain eye contact to show you're actively listening.

2. **Practice Empathy**: Try to understand the speaker's perspective and emotions. Empathizing with their feelings can help build rapport and trust.

3. **Use Nonverbal Cues**: Body language, such as nodding or leaning forward, signals that you're engaged and receptive to what the speaker is saying. It also encourages them to continue sharing.

4. **Ask Open-Ended Questions**: Encourage the speaker to elaborate on their thoughts and feelings by asking open-ended questions. This shows that you're genuinely interested in understanding their perspective.

5. **Paraphrase and Summarize**: After the speaker has finished, paraphrase what they said to ensure you understood correctly. Summarizing the main points demonstrates active listening and helps clarify any misunderstandings.

6. **Avoid Interrupting**: Allow the speaker to finish their thoughts without interruption. Interrupting can disrupt their train of thought and make them feel unheard.

7. **Be Patient**: Sometimes, people need time to gather their thoughts or express themselves fully. Be patient and give them the space they need to communicate effectively.

8. **Provide Feedback**: Offer constructive feedback or validation to show that you've listened and understood what was said. This can help reinforce positive communication and build trust.

9. **Practice Mindfulness**: Stay present in the moment during conversations and avoid letting your mind wander. Mindfulness can help you focus on the speaker and catch subtle cues.

10. **Seek Continuous Improvement**: Reflect on your listening skills regularly and look for areas for improvement. Actively seeking feedback from others can also help you identify blind spots and refine your listening abilities.

By incorporating these strategies into their communication style, workplace leaders can create an environment where employees feel valued, understood, and empowered to contribute their ideas and perspectives.

Assertive Communication

Assertive communication is a style of expressing thoughts, feelings, and needs directly and respectfully without violating the rights of others. It involves stating your opinions, setting boundaries, and advocating for yourself while still considering the feelings and perspectives of others.

Critical components of assertive communication include:

1. **Clarity:** Expressing your thoughts and feelings clearly and directly, without ambiguity.

2. **Respect:** Treating others respectfully by listening actively, acknowledging their viewpoints, and avoiding aggressive or passive-aggressive behavior.

3. **Honesty:** Being honest about your thoughts, feelings, and needs without being overly critical or confrontational.

4. **Confidence:** Assertive communicators have confidence in themselves and their right to express their opinions and needs.

5. **Boundary-setting:** Clearly define personal boundaries and communicate them effectively to others.

6. **Active listening:** Listening to others, understanding their perspectives, and responding thoughtfully.

Practicing assertive communication can lead to healthier relationships, increased self-confidence, and better conflict resolution skills. It's an essential skill in both personal and professional settings.

Giving And Receiving Workplace Feedback

Giving and receiving feedback in the workplace is crucial for personal and professional growth, as well as for the success of the team and organization. Here are some tips for giving and receiving feedback effectively:

Giving Feedback:

1. **Be Specific**: Provide concrete examples to illustrate your points. Vague feedback isn't actionable.

2. **Timely Delivery**: Address issues as soon as possible after they occur while the details are fresh in everyone's mind.

3. **Focus on Behavior, Not Personality**: Frame feedback around actions and outcomes rather than making it personal.

4. **Balance**: Offer both positive and constructive feedback. Acknowledge strengths and achievements as well as areas for improvement.

5. **Be Constructive**: Suggest solutions or alternatives for improvement instead of just pointing out what went wrong.

6. **Ask for Consent**: Before giving feedback, ask if the person is open to receiving it to show respect for their feelings and readiness to listen.

7. **Choose the Right Setting**: Find a private and comfortable setting to discuss feedback. Avoid public or confrontational environments.

8. **Use "I" Statements**: Express your thoughts and feelings rather than make accusatory statements. For example, "I noticed..." instead of "You always..."

Receiving Feedback:

1. **Stay Open-Minded**: Approach feedback with a willingness to learn rather than become defensive.

2. **Listen Actively**: Focus on understanding the feedback without interrupting or becoming defensive. Paraphrase what you heard to ensure you understood correctly.

3. **Seek Clarification**: If something is unclear, ask questions for further explanation. This demonstrates your interest in understanding and improving.

4. **Thank the Giver**: Show appreciation for the feedback, even if it's difficult to hear. Recognize the effort the giver put into providing it.

5. **Reflect**: Take time to reflect on the feedback. Consider how it aligns with your own perceptions and what actions you can take based on it.

6. **Identify Patterns**: Look for recurring themes or patterns in the feedback you receive. This can help you identify areas for focused improvement.

7. **Act on It**: Use the feedback as a basis for growth and development. Set specific goals and actions to address the areas identified for improvement.

8. **Follow-up**: If appropriate, follow up with the feedback giver to discuss progress and any additional support or guidance needed.

By following these guidelines, giving and receiving feedback can become more effective and beneficial for everyone involved, fostering a culture of continuous improvement and growth within the workplace.

Communication Exercise for the Team

Here is a structured communication exercise to help improve the team's interaction and collaboration skills:

Objective:

To enhance listening, clarity, and feedback skills within the team.

Exercise Steps:

1. **Pair Up:**
   - Divide the team into pairs.
   - Each pair will take turns being the speaker and the listener.

2. **Topic Selection:**
   - The speaker will choose a topic related to work (e.g., a recent project, a challenging task, or an idea for improvement).

3. **Speaking:**
   - The speaker talks about the chosen topic for **5 minutes** without interruption.
   - Focus on **clarity** and **conciseness**.

4. **Listening:**
   - The listener pays close attention without interrupting.
   - After the speaker finishes, the listener will **summarize** what they heard in their own words.

5. **Feedback:**
   - The speaker will then provide feedback on the listener's summary, pointing out any missed or misunderstood points.
   - This helps in understanding how well the message was communicated and received.

6. **Switch Roles:**
   - Repeat the process with the roles reversed.

7. **Group Discussion:**
   - After both rounds, reconvene as a group.
   - Each pair shares their experience, focusing on:
     - What was challenging?
     - What worked well?
     - How can communication be improved?

Tips for Effective Communication:

- **Active Listening:** Pay full attention, make eye contact, and avoid thinking about your response while the other person is speaking.
- **Clarification:** Don't hesitate to ask questions if something needs clarification.
- **Feedback:** Provide constructive feedback that is specific and actionable.

Benefits:

- **Improved Understanding:** Enhances the ability to understand and convey messages accurately.
- **Stronger Relationships:** Builds trust and rapport among team members.

- **Enhanced Collaboration:** Facilitates better teamwork and collaboration.

Regularly implementing this exercise can improve the team's communication skills, leading to more effective and efficient interactions.

Building and Leading Teams

Building and leading teams is a multifaceted endeavor requiring skills, strategies, and interpersonal finesse. Here are some key principles to consider:

1. **Clear Vision and Goals**: As a leader, it's crucial to articulate a clear vision for the team's objectives and goals. This provides direction and purpose, aligning everyone's efforts towards a common target.

2. **Recruitment and Diversity**: Building a successful team starts with recruiting the right individuals. Look for diverse skill sets, perspectives, and backgrounds that complement each other. A diverse team fosters creativity, innovation, and adaptability.

3. **Communication**: Effective communication is the cornerstone of team cohesion. Encourage open, honest, and transparent communication channels. Listen actively to your team members and provide regular feedback to ensure everyone is on the same page.

4. **Empowerment and Trust**: Empower your team members by delegating tasks and giving them autonomy to make decisions within their areas of expertise. Trusting your team fosters a sense of ownership and responsibility, increasing motivation and productivity.

5. **Conflict Resolution**: Conflict is inevitable in any team environment. As a leader, it's essential to address conflicts promptly and constructively. Encourage respectful dialogue, seek

compromise, and facilitate resolution to maintain a positive team dynamic.

6. **Continuous Learning and Development**: Foster a culture of continuous learning and development within your team. Provide opportunities for skill enhancement, training, and mentorship. Encourage knowledge sharing and collaboration to foster personal and professional growth.

7. **Recognition and Appreciation**: Recognize and appreciate your team members' contributions and achievements. Celebrate successes, no matter how small, and show genuine appreciation for their efforts. This cultivates a positive work environment and reinforces a sense of belonging and camaraderie.

8. **Adaptability and Resilience**: In today's dynamic business landscape, adaptability and resilience are essential qualities for leaders and team members. Encourage flexibility, embrace change, and learn from setbacks to continuously improve and thrive in challenging situations.

9. **Lead by Example**: As a leader, your actions speak louder than words. Lead by example by demonstrating integrity, accountability, and commitment to the team's values and objectives. Your behavior sets the tone for the entire team and influences their attitudes and actions.

10. **Celebrate Diversity and Inclusion**: Embrace diversity and inclusion within your team. Create an environment where everyone feels valued, respected, and included, regardless of their background or identity. Leverage each team member's unique strengths and perspectives to drive innovation and success.

By focusing on these principles, you can effectively build and lead high-performing teams equipped to tackle challenges, achieve goals, and drive success.

Team Dynamics

Team dynamics in the workplace refer to the way individuals within a team interact with each other, collaborate, and work together to achieve common goals. These dynamics can significantly impact productivity, morale, creativity, and overall team performance. Here are some critical aspects of team dynamics:

1.   **Communication:** Effective communication is essential for smooth team dynamics. Teams need to communicate openly, honestly, and respectfully. Clear communication ensures that everyone understands their roles, responsibilities, and goals, leading to better coordination and collaboration.

2.   **Trust:** Trust is the foundation of strong team dynamics. Team members must trust each other's intentions, competence, and reliability. When trust is present, team members feel comfortable sharing ideas, taking risks, and admitting mistakes, fostering collaboration and innovation.

3.   **Leadership:** Effective leadership is crucial in shaping team dynamics. A good leader sets clear expectations, provides guidance and support, and fosters a positive work environment. They empower team members, encourage participation, and resolve conflicts promptly to maintain harmony within the team.

4.   **Diversity:** Diversity in skills, backgrounds, and perspectives enriches team dynamics by bringing different ideas and approaches. Embracing diversity fosters creativity, enhances problem-solving capabilities, and promotes a culture of inclusion and acceptance within the team.

5.   **Conflict Resolution:** Conflicts are inevitable in any team, but how they are resolved can strengthen or weaken team dynamics. Effective conflict resolution involves addressing issues promptly, listening to all perspectives, finding common ground, and reaching

a mutually acceptable solution. Constructive conflict resolution promotes understanding, trust, and cohesion within the team.

6. **Collaboration:** Successful teams collaborate seamlessly, leveraging each member's strengths to achieve common goals. Collaboration involves sharing resources, knowledge, and expertise, supporting each other's efforts, and working towards shared objectives. When team members collaborate effectively, they accomplish more together than they could individually.

7. **Recognition and Feedback:** Recognizing and appreciating team members' contributions fosters a positive team dynamic. Providing regular feedback helps individuals understand their strengths and areas for improvement, promotes continuous learning and development, and reinforces a culture of accountability and excellence.

8. **Adaptability:** In today's fast-paced work environment, teams must be adaptable and flexible to navigate change effectively. Adaptable teams embrace new challenges, learn from failures, and adjust their strategies to stay aligned with evolving objectives and circumstances.

By fostering positive team dynamics through effective communication, trust, leadership, diversity, conflict resolution, collaboration, recognition, and adaptability, organizations can create high-performing teams capable of achieving their goals and driving success.

Team Building Strategies

Team building is essential for fostering a positive work environment and enhancing productivity. Here are some effective strategies for building strong teams in the workplace:

1. **Clear Goals and Expectations**: Ensure every team member understands their goals and individual roles and responsibilities.

Clarity fosters alignment and helps everyone work towards a common objective.

2. **Effective Communication**: Encourage open and transparent communication among team members. This includes active listening, giving and receiving feedback constructively, and fostering an environment where everyone feels comfortable expressing their ideas and concerns.

3. **Promote Collaboration**: Create opportunities for collaboration through team projects, brainstorming sessions, and cross-functional initiatives. Encourage sharing knowledge and skills among team members to leverage everyone's strengths.

4. **Trust-Building Activities**: Organize team-building activities such as outdoor retreats, workshops, or volunteer activities. These activities help foster trust, improve communication, and strengthen relationships among team members.

5. **Celebrate Successes**: Acknowledge and celebrate team achievements, both big and small. Recognizing individual and team contributions boosts morale and reinforces a sense of accomplishment and camaraderie.

6. **Encourage Diversity and Inclusion**: Embrace diversity within the team and create an inclusive environment where everyone feels valued and respected. Different perspectives and experiences enrich the team and contribute to innovative solutions.

7. **Promote Team Bonding**: Encourage social interactions among team members through informal gatherings, team lunches, or virtual coffee breaks. Building personal connections outside of work strengthens team cohesion and fosters a sense of belonging.

8. **Continuous Learning and Development**: Provide opportunities for ongoing learning and skill development through training programs, workshops, or mentorship initiatives. Investing

in employees' growth enhances their capabilities and reinforces their commitment to the team.

9. **Lead by Example**: Leaders play a crucial role in shaping team dynamics. Lead by example by demonstrating integrity, empathy, and accountability. Show appreciation for your team members' efforts and provide support when needed.

10. **Regular Check-ins and Feedback Sessions**: Schedule regular check-ins to discuss progress, address challenges, and provide feedback. These sessions promote accountability, keep everyone aligned, and provide opportunities for continuous improvement.

By implementing these strategies, you can create a cohesive, high-performing team that thrives in the workplace.

Leading High-Performance Teams in The Workplace

Leading high-performance teams in the workplace involves effective communication, fostering a positive team culture, setting clear goals, providing support and resources, and empowering team members to excel. Here are some strategies:

1. **Clear Vision and Goals**: Define a clear vision and set specific, achievable goals for the team. Make sure everyone understands their role in achieving these objectives.

2. **Effective Communication**: Encourage open communication among team members. Foster an environment where members can freely share ideas and feedback is welcomed. Use various communication channels effectively, including meetings, emails, and collaboration tools.

3. **Strength-based Approach**: Understand each team member's strengths and leverage them effectively. Assign tasks that align with their skills and interests to maximize productivity and job satisfaction.

4. **Empowerment and Autonomy**: Provide team members the autonomy to make decisions and take ownership of their work. Trusting your team members to do their jobs well can boost morale and motivation.

5. **Continuous Learning and Development**: Support ongoing learning and development opportunities for team members. Please encourage them to acquire new skills and knowledge relevant to their roles.

6. **Recognition and Reward**: Acknowledge and appreciate team members' efforts and achievements. Publicly recognize individual and team successes and provide appropriate rewards or incentives.

7. **Conflict Resolution**: Address conflicts and disagreements promptly and constructively. Encourage open dialogue to resolve issues and foster a positive team dynamic.

8. **Lead by Example**: Set a positive example through your actions and behaviors. Demonstrate professionalism, integrity, and a strong work ethic to inspire and motivate your team.

9. **Flexibility and Adaptability**: Be flexible and adaptable in your approach to leadership and problem-solving. Respond effectively to changes in the work environment or team dynamics.

10. **Feedback and Performance Management**: Provide regular feedback to team members on their positive and constructive performance. Implement performance management processes to track progress and address any areas for improvement.

11. **Promote Work-Life Balance**: Encourage a healthy work-life balance among team members. Recognize the importance of well-being and support initiatives that promote physical and mental health.

12. **Celebrate Successes**: Celebrate milestones and achievements as a team. This boosts morale and reinforces a sense of accomplishment and camaraderie.

By implementing these strategies, you can effectively lead your team to higher performance levels and achieve success in the workplace.

TEAM BUILDING STRATEGIES

Here's a team-building exercise that's fun and effective in fostering collaboration and communication within a team:

"The Marshmallow Challenge"

Objective: To build the tallest free-standing structure using a set of simple materials.

Materials Needed:

- 20 sticks of spaghetti
- 1 yard of masking tape
- 1 yard of string
- One marshmallow
- Scissors (for cutting tape and string)
- Timer (set to 18 minutes)

Instructions:

1. **Divide into Teams:** Split the participants into small teams of 4-5 people.

2. **Explain the Rules:**
   - Each team has 18 minutes to build the tallest free-standing structure.

- The structure must be able to support the marshmallow on top.
- They can use all or some of the provided materials.

3. **Distribute Materials:** Give each team a set of materials (spaghetti, tape, string, marshmallow).

4. **Start the Timer:** Set the timer for 18 minutes and start the challenge.

5. **Observe:** Walk around and observe how teams are working together. Notice the strategies they employ and how they communicate.

6. **Time's Up:** When the time is up, measure the structures to see which is the tallest and can support the marshmallow.

7. **Debrief:**
   - Discuss what strategies worked and what didn't.
   - Talk about the importance of planning, prototyping, and teamwork.
   - Highlight any innovative approaches taken by the teams.

Learning Outcomes:

- **Collaboration:** Teams must work together, combining their strengths and ideas.
- **Communication:** Clear and effective communication is essential for coordinating efforts and sharing ideas.
- **Problem-solving:** Teams must overcome the challenges of building a stable structure.
- **Creativity:** Encourages out-of-the-box thinking and innovation.

- **Time Management:** Teams must manage their time effectively to complete the task within the limit.

This exercise helps build teamwork and provides insights into group dynamics and individual roles within a team.

Conflict Resolution and Negotiation

Conflict resolution and negotiation are essential skills in the workplace to maintain harmony and achieve mutually beneficial outcomes. Here are some critical strategies for both:

Conflict Resolution:

1. **Address the Issue Promptly**: Ignoring conflicts can escalate the situation. Address conflicts as soon as they arise.

2. **Active Listening**: Listen to all parties involved without interrupting. Understand their perspectives and concerns.

3. **Identify the Underlying Issues**: Often, conflicts arise from deeper issues. Identify these underlying causes to address the root problem.

4. **Stay Calm and Objective**: Emotions can escalate conflicts. Stay calm and focus on finding a solution rather than assigning blame.

5. **Seek Common Ground**: Find areas of agreement and build on them to find a resolution that satisfies all parties involved.

6. **Generate Solutions Together**: Encourage open dialogue and brainstorming to find creative solutions that address everyone's needs.

7. **Use a Mediator if Necessary**: In cases of intense conflict, consider bringing in a neutral third party to facilitate the resolution process.

8. **Follow-up**: After resolving the conflict, follow up to ensure the solution works and address any lingering issues.

Negotiation:

1. **Prepare Thoroughly**: Understand your goals and priorities before entering negotiations. Research the other party's position and interests.

2. **Focus on Interests, Not Positions**: Identify the underlying interests driving each party's position and look for mutually beneficial solutions.

3. **Maintain Flexibility**: Be willing to compromise and explore alternative solutions to reach a mutually acceptable agreement.

4. **Build Rapport**: A positive relationship with the other party can facilitate more productive negotiations.

5. **Communicate Clearly and Assertively**: Communicate your needs, priorities, and concerns while actively listening to the other party.

6. **Use Objective Criteria**: Base decisions on objective criteria rather than personal preferences or power dynamics.

7. **Know When to Walk Away**: Sometimes, the best option is to walk away from a negotiation that is unlikely to result in a satisfactory outcome.

8. **Document Agreements**: Once an agreement occurs, document it in writing to ensure clarity and avoid misunderstandings.

By employing these strategies, individuals can effectively resolve conflicts and negotiate agreements in the workplace, fostering a positive and productive work environment.

Understanding Conflict in The Workplace

Conflict in the workplace is a common occurrence that arises from differences in opinions, goals, personalities, and communication styles among employees. Understanding and managing conflict effectively is crucial for maintaining a healthy and productive work environment. Here are some key points to consider:

1. **Acknowledge its existence**: Ignoring or avoiding conflict only allows it to fester and escalate. Acknowledge conflict when it occurs and address it promptly.

2. **Identify the root cause**: Understanding the underlying reasons for the conflict is essential for finding a resolution. Is it due to a misunderstanding, competing goals, personality clashes, or something else?

3. **Encourage open communication**: Create an environment where employees feel comfortable expressing their concerns and opinions. Encourage active listening and constructive dialogue to facilitate understanding between conflicting parties.

4. **Seek common ground**: Look for areas of agreement or mutual interest that can serve as a basis for resolving the conflict. Finding common ground can help parties work towards a compromise or solution that benefits everyone involved.

5. **Use conflict resolution techniques**: Various strategies and techniques exist for resolving conflicts, such as negotiation, mediation, and compromise. Choose the approach that best suits the situation and the personalities involved.

6. **Focus on solutions, not blame**: Instead of assigning blame or dwelling on past grievances, focus on finding solutions to the current Issue. Keep the discussion forward-looking and goal-oriented.

7. **Set clear expectations**: Clearly communicate expectations regarding behavior, responsibilities, and conflict resolution processes to all employees. Having clear guidelines can help prevent

conflicts and provide a framework for addressing them when they occur.

8.   **Seek outside assistance if necessary**: In some cases, conflicts may be too complex or deeply entrenched to resolve internally. In such situations, seeking the help of a neutral third party, such as a mediator or HR professional, can be beneficial.

9.   **Follow up**: After resolving a conflict, follow up to ensure that the solution works and that any lingering issues are addressed. Monitoring the situation can help prevent the conflict from reigniting.

10. **Learn from the experience**: Conflict can be an opportunity for growth and learning. Encourage employees to reflect on the conflict, identify lessons learned, and apply them to future interactions.

By understanding the nature of conflict and implementing effective conflict resolution strategies, organizations can minimize the negative impact of conflicts and foster a more positive and collaborative work environment.

Conflict Resolution Strategies

Here's a conflict resolution framework tailored for the workplace:

1.   **Define the Issue:** Identify the problem or disagreement. Encourage those involved to express their perspectives without interruptions. Ensure that everyone understands the issue at hand.

2.   **Encourage Open Communication:** Foster an environment where all parties feel comfortable expressing their thoughts and feelings. Active listening is crucial here; ensure everyone feels heard and understood.

3.   **Identify Common Goals:** Find common ground or shared objectives among the conflicting parties. Emphasize the importance of working towards a mutually beneficial solution.

4. **Brainstorm Solutions:** Encourage creative thinking to generate multiple potential solutions. Encourage everyone involved to contribute ideas without judgment.

5. **Evaluate Solutions:** Objectively assess the pros and cons of each proposed solution. Consider factors such as feasibility, impact, and alignment with organizational values.

6. **Agree on a Solution:** Once all options have been considered, work together to select the best solution. Consensus is ideal, but compromise may be necessary. Ensure that everyone commits to implementing the chosen solution.

7. **Implement the Solution:** Develop a plan for the agreed-upon solution. Assign responsibilities and establish timelines as needed. Communication is key throughout this process.

8. **Follow-Up and Evaluate:** Periodically review the solution's effectiveness. Solicit feedback from those involved to determine if any adjustments are necessary. Celebrate successes and address any lingering issues promptly.

9. **Mediation or Escalation:** If the conflict persists despite efforts to resolve it internally, consider involving a neutral third party or escalating the Issue to higher management or HR for further assistance.

Remember, conflict is a natural part of any workplace, but how it's managed can significantly impact productivity and morale. Encouraging open communication, empathy, and collaboration can help turn conflicts into opportunities for growth and strengthen relationships.

Negotiation Techniques for The Workplace

Negotiation in the workplace is a vital skill that can help you advance your career, resolve conflicts, and achieve your goals. Here are some techniques to help you negotiate effectively:

1. **Prepare Thoroughly**: Understand your objectives and limits and research the other party's position. Anticipate potential objections and prepare responses.

2. **Focus on Interests, Not Positions**: Understand both parties' underlying interests rather than just their stated positions. This allows you to find creative solutions that satisfy everyone's needs.

3. **Establish Rapport**: Building a positive relationship with the other party can make negotiations smoother. Listen actively, show empathy, and try to find common ground.

4. **Use Active Listening**: Pay close attention to what the other party is saying and ask clarifying questions to demonstrate understanding. This helps build trust and can uncover valuable information.

5. **Communicate Clearly**: Be articulate and concise in expressing your points. Avoid ambiguity and use language that is easy to understand.

6. **Be Flexible**: While knowing your objectives is essential, be willing to adapt and compromise to reach a mutually beneficial agreement.

7. **Create Value**: Look for opportunities to expand the pie rather than just dividing it. Find ways to add value for both parties through creative solutions or trade-offs.

8. **Maintain a Positive Attitude**: Stay calm and composed, even if negotiations become challenging. A positive attitude can help keep discussions productive and focused on finding solutions.

9. **Know When to Walk Away**: Sometimes, the best option is to walk away from a negotiation that isn't going anywhere or doesn't meet your needs. Clearly understand your alternatives and when it's time to pursue them.

10. **Follow-Up**: Following an agreement, follow through on any commitments. This helps build trust and ensures a positive outcome for both parties.

By incorporating these techniques into your negotiation approach, you can navigate workplace negotiations more effectively and achieve better results.

PART THREE:
ORGANIZATIONAL LEADERSHIP SKILLS

Organizational leadership skills are essential for effectively managing teams and driving success in the workplace. Here's a rundown of some basic skills:

1. **Communication**: Clear and concise communication is crucial for conveying expectations, providing feedback, and fostering collaboration among team members.

2. **Visionary Thinking**: A good leader should be able to articulate a compelling vision for the organization and inspire others to work towards it.

3. **Decision Making**: Leaders must make informed decisions under pressure, considering various factors and potential outcomes.

4. **Problem-solving**: Identifying issues, analyzing root causes, and developing practical solutions are fundamental skills for any leader.

5. **Empathy**: Understanding the perspectives and feelings of team members fosters trust and helps leaders make decisions that consider the well-being of their employees.

6. **Adaptability**: In today's rapidly changing business environment, leaders must be flexible and adapt their strategies to new circumstances.

7. **Delegation**: Effective delegation involves assigning tasks to the right people based on their strengths and skills while providing necessary support and guidance.

8. **Motivation**: Inspiring and motivating team members to perform at their best requires understanding their goals and providing meaningful incentives and recognition.

9. **Conflict Resolution**: Addressing conflicts promptly and diplomatically is essential for maintaining a positive work environment and fostering healthy relationships among team members.

10. **Strategic Planning**: Leaders should be able to set clear goals, develop action plans, and allocate resources effectively to achieve long-term success.

11. **Empowerment**: Giving employees autonomy and opportunities for growth empowers them to take ownership of their work and contribute more effectively to the organization.

12. **Ethical Leadership**: Upholding ethical standards and acting with integrity builds trust and credibility within and with external stakeholders.

13. **Team Building**: Creating a cohesive and high-performing team involves fostering collaboration, encouraging diversity of thought, and celebrating collective achievements.

14. **Feedback**: Providing constructive feedback and actively seeking input from team members helps individuals grow professionally and fosters a culture of continuous improvement.

15. **Resilience**: Leaders should be able to bounce back from setbacks, learn from failures, and maintain a positive outlook in challenging situations.

Developing these skills takes time and practice, but investing in honing them can significantly enhance one's effectiveness as a workplace leader.

Strategic Thinking and Planning for the Workplace

Strategic thinking and planning are crucial components of effective leadership and organizational success in the workplace. Here's a breakdown of crucial steps and considerations:

1. **Vision and Mission Statement**: Clearly define the organization's purpose and long-term goals. The vision outlines what the organization aspires to achieve, while the mission defines its core purpose and how it will accomplish its objectives.

2. **SWOT Analysis**: Conduct a thorough analysis of the organization's strengths, weaknesses, opportunities, and threats (SWOT). This analysis helps understand internal capabilities and external factors that may impact the organization's strategy.

3. **Setting Objectives**: Based on the analysis, set specific, measurable, achievable, relevant, and time-bound (SMART) objectives. These objectives should align with the organization's mission and vision.

4. **Strategy Formulation**: Develop strategies to achieve the objectives identified in the previous step. This involves determining the best action to leverage strengths, mitigate weaknesses, seize opportunities, and counter threats.

5. **Resource Allocation**: Strategically allocate resources, including finances, workforce, and time, to support the implementation of the chosen strategies. Prioritize initiatives based on their potential impact on organizational goals.

6. **Action Planning**: Create detailed action plans outlining the steps, timelines, responsibilities, and resources required to execute each strategy effectively. Review and adjust these plans regularly as needed to adapt to changing circumstances.

7. **Monitoring and Evaluation**: Implement mechanisms to monitor progress towards objectives and evaluate the effectiveness of strategies. Key performance indicators (KPIs) should be established to track performance and measure success.

8. **Risk Management**: Identify potential risks and develop mitigation strategies. Regularly assess risks and update risk management plans to ensure the organization can respond effectively to unexpected challenges.

9. **Communication and Alignment**: Ensure clear communication of the strategic plan throughout the organization to foster alignment

and engagement at all levels. Employees should understand how their roles contribute to the overall strategy.

10. **Continuous Improvement**: Encourage continuous improvement by regularly reviewing and refining the strategic plan based on feedback, lessons learned, and internal and external environment changes.

By following these steps and integrating strategic thinking and planning into the workplace culture, organizations can better adapt to change, capitalize on opportunities, and achieve long-term objectives.

The Strategic Planning Process for The Workplace

Developing a strategic plan for the workplace involves several vital steps to ensure alignment with organizational goals and effective implementation. Here's a structured approach you might consider:

1. **Define Vision and Mission:**

Start by articulating the organization's vision (long-term goal) and mission (purpose). These statements provide direction and purpose for the strategic plan.

2. **Assess Current State:**

Conduct a thorough analysis of the organization's current state, including strengths, weaknesses, opportunities, and threats (SWOT analysis). This assessment helps identify areas for improvement and potential challenges.

3. **Set Objectives and Goals**: Based on the assessment, set specific, measurable, achievable, relevant, and time-bound (SMART) objectives and goals that directly support the organization's mission and vision.

4. **Develop Strategies:**

Determine the strategies needed to achieve the objectives and goals. Consider different approaches and tactics that leverage the organization's strengths and address its weaknesses.

5. **Allocate Resources:**

Identify the resources (financial, human, technological, etc.) required to implement the strategies effectively and ensure that resources support the strategic initiatives.

6. **Create Action Plans:**

Break down the strategies into actionable steps and create detailed action plans. Assign responsibilities, set deadlines, and establish key performance indicators (KPIs) to track progress.

7. **Communicate and Engage:**

Communicate the strategic plan to all stakeholders, including employees, management, and external partners. Ensure that everyone understands their roles and responsibilities in achieving the objectives.

8. **Implement and Monitor:**

Implement the action plans according to the established timelines. Continuously monitor progress against the set objectives and be prepared to adapt strategies as needed based on feedback and changing circumstances.

9. **Evaluate and Adjust:**

Regularly evaluate the strategic plan's effectiveness by measuring performance against KPIs and objectives. Identify areas of success and areas that require improvement and adjust the plan accordingly.

10. **Sustain and Review:**

Ensure the strategic plan remains relevant and aligned with the organization's evolving needs and external environment. Conduct periodic reviews to assess progress, make necessary adjustments, and ensure long-term sustainability.

Following these steps, you can develop a comprehensive strategic plan that guides decision-making, fosters organizational alignment, and drives workplace success.

Creating a Vision and Mission in The Workplace

Crafting a clear vision and mission for your workplace is essential for providing your team direction, alignment, and inspiration. Here's a breakdown of each and some tips on how to create them effectively:

Vision Statement:

What is it?

A vision statement outlines the organization's desired future state or goal. It's a concise declaration of where you aim to be in the long term.

Key characteristics:

Aspirational: It should inspire and motivate employees.

Future-oriented: Focus on where the organization is headed.

Clear and memorable: Easily understood and communicated.

Example: "To be the global leader in sustainable technology solutions, driving positive environmental and societal change."

Mission Statement:

What is it?

A mission statement defines the organization's purpose, reason for existence, and core values. It answers the question, "What do we do, and why do we do it?"

Key characteristics:

Specific and actionable: Describes what the organization does and how it does it.

Reflects core values: Aligns with the principles and beliefs of the organization.

Realistic: Achievable within the organization's capabilities.

Example: "Our mission is to provide innovative and reliable software solutions that empower businesses to thrive in a rapidly changing digital landscape while fostering a culture of creativity, collaboration, and integrity."

Tips for creating them:

1. **Involve stakeholders:** Seek input from employees, leadership, and other stakeholders to ensure buy-in and alignment.

2. **Reflect on core values:** Identify the fundamental beliefs and principles that guide your organization.

3. **Be concise:** Keep both statements brief and to the point for easy understanding and memorability.

4. **Consider your audience:** Tailor the language and tone to resonate with employees, customers, and other stakeholders.

5. **Ensure alignment:** Both statements should complement each other and align with the organization's goals and values.

6. **Review and refine:** Regularly revisit your vision and mission statements to ensure they remain relevant and reflect the organization's evolving needs and aspirations.

Creating a compelling vision and mission statement gives your team a clear sense of purpose and direction, fostering a shared understanding of the organization's goals and values.

Implementing Strategic Initiatives in The Workplace

Implementing strategic initiatives in the workplace requires careful planning, communication, and execution. Here's a step-by-step guide to help you navigate this process:

1. **Understand the Strategic Objectives**: Before implementing any initiatives, clearly understand your organization's strategic objectives. These could include increasing market share, improving customer satisfaction, or reducing operational costs.

2. **Identify Key Initiatives**: Once you understand the strategic objectives, identify the key initiatives that will help you achieve them. These initiatives should directly align with the organization's overall goals.

3. **Create a Project Plan**: Develop a detailed plan for each initiative, outlining the objectives, timeline, budget, resources required, and critical milestones. Break down each initiative into smaller tasks to make it more manageable.

4. **Allocate Resources**: Ensure you have the necessary resources—such as budget, personnel, and Technology—allocated to support implementing each initiative, which may involve reallocating existing resources or acquiring new ones.

5. **Communicate Effectively**: Communication is critical throughout the implementation process. Communicate the strategic objectives, the rationale behind the initiatives, and how they align

with the organization's goals to all stakeholders, including employees, managers, and external partners.

6.   **Gain Buy-in**: Getting buy-in from all stakeholders is essential to ensure their support and commitment to the initiatives. Address any concerns or objections they may have and emphasize the potential benefits of the initiatives for both the organization and individual stakeholders.

7.   **Empower Employees**: Empower employees to take ownership of the initiatives by providing them with the necessary training, resources, and authority to execute their roles effectively. Encourage collaboration and foster a culture of innovation and continuous improvement.

8.   **Monitor Progress**: Regularly monitor and evaluate each initiative's progress against the established milestones and objectives. Identify any obstacles or challenges and take corrective action to keep the initiatives on track.

9.   **Adapt and Iterate**: Be flexible and willing to adapt your approach based on feedback and changing circumstances. Continuously gather insights and learnings from the implementation process and use them to refine your strategies and improve future initiatives.

10. **Celebrate Successes**: Recognize and celebrate the achievements and milestones reached throughout the implementation process. This helps boost morale, reinforces the importance of the initiatives, and motivates stakeholders to continue their efforts.

By following these steps and maintaining a strategic focus, you can effectively implement initiatives that drive your organization toward its long-term goals.

Change Management in The Workplace

Change management in the workplace refers to the structured approach organizations take to transition individuals, teams, and the organization from a current state to a desired future state. It involves careful planning, communication, and implementation to ensure that changes are smoothly adopted and effectively integrated into the organization's culture and operations.

Here are some key elements and best practices of change management:

1. **Clear Vision and Objectives**: Clearly define the change initiative's purpose and goals. Communicate these objectives to all stakeholders to ensure alignment and understanding.

2. **Stakeholder Engagement**: Identify all stakeholders impacted by the change and involve them in the process. Solicit their input, address concerns, and keep them informed throughout the change process.

3. **Communication**: Effective communication is crucial for managing change. Provide regular updates on the progress of the change initiative, address any uncertainties or resistance, and celebrate milestones to maintain morale.

4. **Change Leadership**: Strong leadership is essential to guide the organization through change. Leaders should demonstrate commitment to the change, provide direction, and support employees through the transition.

5. **Employee Involvement**: Encourage employee involvement and participation in the change process. Solicit feedback, involve employees in decision-making where appropriate, and provide opportunities for training and development to build necessary skills.

6. **Training and Support**: Ensure employees have the knowledge and resources to adapt to the changes. Offer training programs,

workshops, and support systems to help employees develop new skills and behaviors.

7. **Risk Management**: Identify potential risks and challenges associated with the change and develop strategies to mitigate them. Anticipate resistance and develop contingency plans to address it.

8. **Monitor and Evaluate**: Continuously monitor the progress of the change initiative and evaluate its effectiveness. Collect stakeholder feedback, analyze performance metrics, and adjust as needed to ensure successful implementation.

9. **Celebrate Successes**: Acknowledge and celebrate successes to maintain momentum and morale. Recognize the efforts of individuals and teams contributing to the change initiative's success.

By incorporating these elements into the change management process, organizations can increase the likelihood of successful change implementation and minimize disruptions to the workplace.

Understanding Change in The Workplace

Understanding change in the workplace is essential for navigating transitions, fostering adaptability, and ensuring organizational success. Change can manifest in various forms, including technological advancements, organizational restructuring, market dynamics shifts, or leadership changes.

Here are some key aspects to consider when understanding change in the workplace:

Change Drivers: Identify the factors prompting change. These could include internal drivers such as a need for innovation or external factors like market competition or regulatory requirements.

1. **Communication**: Effective communication is crucial during times of change. Leaders should clearly articulate the reasons for change, the intended outcomes, and how it will impact

employees. Encouraging open dialogue and addressing concerns help alleviate uncertainty.

2. **Resilience and Adaptability**: Encouraging resilience and adaptability among employees can help them navigate change more effectively. Providing resources for skill development, fostering a growth mindset, and offering support networks can bolster resilience.

3. **Change Management Strategies**: Implementing structured change management strategies can help facilitate smooth transitions. This may involve creating a roadmap, setting clear goals, involving stakeholders, and regularly evaluating progress.

4. **Employee Involvement**: Involving employees in the change process can increase buy-in and foster a sense of ownership. Soliciting feedback, involving employees in decision-making, and recognizing their contributions can help create a more positive change experience.

5. **Training and Development**: Equip employees with the skills and knowledge to adapt to new systems or processes. Providing training programs, workshops, and mentorship opportunities can help mitigate resistance to change.

6. **Leadership Support**: Strong leadership is vital for guiding teams through change. Leaders should demonstrate empathy, provide support, and serve as role models for embracing change.

7. **Monitoring and Adaptation**: Continuously monitor the change process and be prepared to adapt strategies as needed. Soliciting feedback, measuring progress against objectives, and accordingly adjusting can help ensure successful outcomes.

8. **Celebrating Success**: Recognize milestones achieved throughout the change process. Acknowledging accomplishments can boost morale and reinforce the benefits of embracing change.

By understanding and proactively addressing these aspects of change in the workplace, organizations can navigate transitions more effectively and position themselves for long-term success.

Managing Resistance to Change in The Workplace

Managing resistance to change in the workplace is crucial for ensuring smooth transitions and successful implementation of new initiatives. Here are some strategies to effectively address resistance to change:

1. **Communicate Effectively**: Transparent and frequent communication is essential. Clearly explain the reasons for the change, the expected benefits, and how it will impact individuals and the organization. Address concerns and provide opportunities for employees to ask questions and share their thoughts.

2. **Involve Employees**: Involve employees in the change process by seeking their input and feedback. When people feel they have a say in decisions that affect them, they are more likely to support the change. Encourage participation in planning and problem-solving sessions.

3. **Provide Training and Support**: Offer training and support to help employees develop the skills and knowledge needed to adapt to the change successfully. This can reduce anxiety and increase their confidence in navigating the transition.

4. **Address Concerns**: Take the time to listen to employees' concerns and address them thoughtfully. Understand the reasons behind their resistance and provide reassurance where possible. Be empathetic and acknowledge the challenges they may be facing.

5.   **Lead by Example**: Leaders play a crucial role in managing change. Demonstrate your commitment to the change by modeling the desired behaviors and attitudes. Show resilience in the face of challenges and remain optimistic about the future.

6.   **Celebrate Successes**: Acknowledge and celebrate small wins along the way. Recognizing progress helps build momentum and motivates employees to continue working toward embracing change.

7.   **Provide Resources**: Ensure employees can access the resources and support needed to adapt to the change. This may include additional training, coaching, or other forms of assistance.

8.   **Address Resistance Proactively**: Anticipate potential sources of resistance and address them proactively. Develop strategies for mitigating resistance before it becomes a significant barrier to progress.

9.   **Foster a Culture of Continuous Improvement**: Encourage a culture where employees see change as an ordinary and necessary part of business. Foster an environment where employees feel empowered to suggest and implement changes that improve processes and outcomes.

10. **Monitor and Adjust**: Continuously monitor the progress of the change initiative and be prepared to make adjustments as needed. Solicit feedback from employees and stakeholders and use this information to refine your approach.

By employing these strategies, organizations can effectively manage resistance to change and increase the likelihood of successful outcomes.

Leading Organizational Change

Leading organizational change in the workplace requires strategic planning, effective communication, and strong leadership skills. Here are some steps to guide you through the process:

1. **Assessment and Planning**: Begin by assessing the organization's current state thoroughly. Identify areas that need improvement or change and determine the goals you want to achieve through the change process. Develop a clear plan outlining the steps you will take to implement the changes.

2. **Create a Vision**: Develop a compelling vision for the organization's future. Communicate this vision to all stakeholders, including employees, managers, and other relevant parties. Help everyone understand why change is necessary and how it will benefit the organization in the long run.

3. **Build a Coalition**: Gain support for the change initiative by building a coalition of key organizational stakeholders and influencers. This could include respected senior leaders, managers, and employees who influence others. Engage them early in the process and involve them in decision-making to foster ownership and commitment to the change.

4. **Communication**: Effective communication is crucial throughout the change process. Be transparent about the reasons for the change, the expected outcomes, and how it will impact employees. Provide regular updates, address concerns and questions, and actively solicit employee feedback to ensure their voices are heard.

5. **Empower and Support Employees**: Empower employees to be active participants in the change process by involving them in decision-making, soliciting their input, and

providing opportunities for skill development and training. Offer support to help employees navigate the transition period and address any concerns or resistance.

6. **Lead by Example**: As a leader, it's essential to lead by example and demonstrate your commitment to the change initiative. Model the behaviors and attitudes you want to see in others, be open to feedback, and be willing to adapt your approach as needed.

7. **Manage Resistance**: Anticipate and address resistance to change proactively. Listen to concerns and address them respectfully. Provide a rationale for the change and involve employees in finding solutions. Celebrate small wins along the way to maintain momentum and keep people motivated.

8. **Monitor Progress and Adjust**: Continuously monitor progress towards the desired outcomes and be prepared to adjust your approach as needed. Stay flexible and responsive to changes in the internal and external environment, and be willing to iterate on your plans to ensure success.

By following these steps and demonstrating strong leadership, you can effectively lead organizational change and drive positive outcomes for your organization.

Coaching and Mentoring in The Workplace

Coaching and mentoring in the workplace are invaluable tools for personal and professional development. Here's a breakdown of each:

Coaching involves a structured and goal-oriented approach to helping individuals improve specific skills or achieve objectives. It typically focuses on short-term goals and is often task-oriented. Coaches provide feedback, guidance, and support to enhance performance and unlock potential. Coaching sessions may involve skill-building exercises, role-playing, or action plans to address areas for improvement.

Mentoring, on the other hand, is a more long-term and relationship-focused process. Mentors offer guidance, wisdom, and support based on their experiences to help mentees navigate their careers and personal development. Mentoring relationships are often less structured than coaching and can encompass a broader range of topics, including career advancement, work-life balance, and personal growth. Mentors are trusted advisors who provide encouragement, perspective, and networking opportunities.

Both coaching and mentoring play vital roles in fostering a culture of continuous learning and growth within organizations. They empower individuals to reach their full potential, enhance performance, and achieve their career aspirations. Additionally, they contribute to building stronger teams and fostering a supportive and collaborative work environment.

Coaching vs. Mentoring

Coaching and mentoring are often interchangeable but refer to distinct personal and professional development approaches.

Coaching typically involves a structured process where a coach assists individuals or groups in achieving specific goals. Coaches use various techniques to help clients identify their strengths, weaknesses, and obstacles and then work with them to develop strategies for improvement. Coaching often focuses on short-term objectives, such as improving performance in a particular area, enhancing leadership skills, or navigating career transitions. Coaches may have little experience in the client's field but are skilled in asking powerful questions and guiding the client toward solutions.

Mentoring, on the other hand, is a more informal and relationship-driven process. A mentor is typically someone with more experience and expertise in a particular field who provides guidance, support, and advice to a less experienced individual, a mentee. Unlike coaching, mentoring is often long-term and involves sharing knowledge, insights, and personal experiences to help the mentee develop professionally and personally. Mentors may offer career advice, share industry insights, and provide networking opportunities to help mentees advance.

In summary, coaching focuses on achieving specific goals through a structured process, while mentoring emphasizes long-term relationship building and guidance based on the mentor's experience and expertise. Depending on the individual's needs and objectives, both approaches can be valuable for personal and professional development.

Developing Coaching Skills

Coaching skills for the workplace can greatly enhance your ability to support and develop your team members. Here's a roadmap to develop those skills:

1. **Understand Coaching Principles**: Familiarize yourself with the principles of coaching. Understand that coaching is about helping individuals unlock their potential through self-discovery and guided questioning rather than just giving advice.

2. **Active Listening**: Practice listening to understand your team members' perspectives. This involves giving your full attention, paraphrasing what they say to ensure understanding, and asking clarifying questions.

3. **Empathy and Emotional Intelligence**: Cultivate empathy and emotional intelligence to connect with your team members on a deeper level. Understand their emotions and perspectives, and tailor your coaching approach accordingly.

4. **Questioning Skills**: Learn to ask powerful questions that encourage reflection and self-discovery. Open-ended questions such

as "What do you think the best course of action is?" or "How do you feel about that?" can prompt deeper thinking.

5. **Feedback Skills**: Develop the ability to give constructive feedback effectively. Focus on specific behaviors, offer observations rather than judgments, and suggest actionable steps for improvement.

6. **Goal Setting and Action Planning**: Help your team members set SMART (Specific, Measurable, Achievable, Relevant, Time-bound) goals and develop action plans to achieve them. Guide them in breaking down larger goals into manageable steps.

7. **Building Trust**: Establish trust with your team members. Be honest, reliable, and supportive. Trust is essential for open communication and receptivity to coaching.

8. **Adaptability**: Recognize that each team member is unique and may require a different coaching approach. Be adaptable and flexible in your coaching style to meet individual needs.

9. **Practice Self-Reflection**: Continuously reflect on your coaching interactions. Identify areas for improvement and celebrate successes. Self-awareness is critical to becoming a more effective coach.

10. **Seek Feedback and Training**: Actively seek feedback from your team members and colleagues on your coaching efforts. Additionally, consider attending workshops, reading books, or taking courses on coaching to deepen your knowledge and skills.

11. **Apply Coaching in Real Scenarios**: Look for opportunities to apply your coaching skills in real workplace scenarios. Practice coaching during one-on-one meetings, performance reviews, or when helping team members overcome challenges.

12. **Patience and Persistence**: Developing coaching skills takes time and practice. Be patient with yourself and persistent in your

efforts to improve. Over time, you'll become more confident and effective as a workplace coach.

How To Conduct a Coaching Session

Conducting a coaching session involves several structured steps designed to facilitate employee growth, development, and goal achievement. Here's a detailed guide on how to perform a successful coaching session:

1. Preparation: Review previous notes or sessions to understand the employee's background, goals, and progress.

1. **Set the Agenda**: Have a clear agenda and objectives for the session. This can include topics to discuss, goals to achieve, and specific focus areas.

2. Building Rapport

1. **Warm Welcome**: Begin with a friendly greeting to make the employee feel comfortable.

2. **Check-In**: Start with a brief check-in to understand the employee's current mind. Ask about their week, any significant events, or how they feel.

3. Setting the Stage

1. **Review Objectives**: Clarify the session objectives. Reiterate the coaching goals and how today's session fits into the larger picture.

2. **Establish Confidentiality**: Remind the employee that the session is confidential to build trust and openness.

4. Active Listening

1. **Listen Attentively**: Focus on the employee's words, tone, and body language. Avoid interrupting and let them express themselves fully.

2. **Ask Open-Ended Questions**: Use questions encouraging deep thinking and exploration, such as "What challenges are you facing?" or "How do you feel about this situation?"

5. Exploration and Insight

- **Identify Issues**: Help employees identify their core issues or challenges.

- **Encourage Reflection**: Prompt employees to reflect on their experiences, thoughts, and feelings. Use reflective questions like "What did you learn from this experience?" or "How does this align with your personal goals?"

6. Goal Setting

1. **Define SMART Goals**: Ensure the employee's goals are Specific, Measurable, Achievable, Relevant, and Time-bound.

2. **Action Planning**: Develop a clear action plan with steps the employee can take to achieve their goals. Discuss potential obstacles and how to overcome them.

7. Providing feedback

1. **Constructive Feedback**: Offer specific, actionable feedback focused on behavior rather than personality. Use the "sandwich" method: start with a positive, discuss areas for improvement, and end with another positive.

2. **Encourage Self-Feedback**: Ask employees to evaluate their performance and growth areas.

8. Accountability

1. **Set Milestones**: Agree on specific milestones and deadlines to track progress.

2. **Follow-up**: Plan for follow-up sessions to review progress and adjust the action plan as needed.

9. Conclusion

1. **Summarize the Session**: Recap the key points discussed, the goals set, and the action plan.

2. **End on a Positive Note**: Reinforce the employee's strengths and express confidence in their ability to achieve their goals.

3. **Schedule Next Session**: Arrange the date and time for the next coaching session.

10. Post-Session Activities

1. **Document the Session**: Take detailed notes of discussed topics, the goals set, and the action plan.

2. **Reflect on Your Performance**: Consider what went well in the session and what could be improved next time.

3. **Follow-up with the employee**: After the coaching session, the employee may have thoughts or questions regarding the session. Give them another chance to ask questions or seek clarification.

Tips for Effective Coaching

1. **Be Empathetic**: Show genuine care and understanding for the employee's situation.

2. **Maintain Professionalism**: Keep a balance between being friendly and maintaining professional boundaries.

3. **Stay Flexible**: Be prepared to adapt your approach based on the employee's needs and responses during the session.

4. **Continuous Learning**: Stay updated with new techniques and tools to enhance your coaching practice.

By following these steps and maintaining a supportive and goal-oriented approach, you can conduct practical coaching sessions that facilitate meaningful progress for your employees.

Fostering a Culture of Mentorship in The Workplace

Fostering a culture of mentorship within an organization can be incredibly beneficial for individual growth and overall team performance. Here are some steps to cultivate this culture:

1. **Lead by Example:** Leaders should actively participate in mentorship programs and demonstrate their commitment to mentoring others. When leaders are seen as mentors, it sets a powerful example for everyone else.

2. **Provide Resources:** Ensure mentorship programs have resources, such as training materials, guidelines, and support networks. This can help mentors and mentees navigate their roles more effectively.

3. **Promote Open Communication:** Encourage open dialogue between mentors and mentees. Create a safe space for mentees to ask questions, seek advice, and provide feedback. Effective communication is crucial for a successful mentorship relationship.

4. **Match Mentors with Mentees:** Take the time to match mentors and mentees thoughtfully based on their goals, experiences, and personalities. A good match increases the likelihood of a productive and meaningful mentorship relationship.

5. **Set Clear Expectations:** Define the mentorship program's goals and expectations upfront. This includes the frequency of meetings, topics to be discussed, and desired outcomes. Clarity helps both mentors and mentees stay focused and motivated.

6. **Encourage Personal Development:** Mentors should help mentees set and achieve personal development goals. Mentorship should focus on professional growth as well as personal growth and well-being.

7. **Recognize and Reward Participation:** Acknowledge and celebrate the efforts of both mentors and mentees. Recognition can be in the form of awards, public praise, or other incentives to show appreciation for their commitment to mentorship.

8. **Measure Impact:** Regularly evaluate the mentorship program's effectiveness. Collect feedback from participants to identify areas for improvement and adjust as needed.

9. **Promote Continuity:** Encourage long-term mentorship relationships to promote continuity and ongoing support. Some mentorship connections may naturally evolve into lifelong professional relationships.

10. **Embed Mentorship in the Culture:** Make mentorship an integral part of the organization's culture by integrating it into other initiatives such as onboarding, leadership development programs, and performance reviews.

By implementing these strategies, organizations can foster a culture of mentorship that supports continuous learning, growth, and collaboration among employees.

A workplace mentorship culture can significantly enhance employee development, engagement, and retention. Here's a comprehensive guide to fostering such a culture:

1. Leadership Buy-In and Support

1. **Executive Sponsorship**: Secure commitment from top management to champion the mentorship program.

2. **Role Modeling**: Encourage leaders to participate as mentors and actively demonstrate the value of mentorship.

2. Clear Objectives and Goals

1. **Define Purpose**: Clearly articulate the mentorship program's goals (e.g., career development, skill enhancement, onboarding support).

2. **Align with Organizational Goals**: Ensure the mentorship program supports the organization's broader objectives.

3. Structured Program Design

1. **Mentorship Models**: Decide on the types of mentorship (e.g., one-on-one, group, peer, reverse mentoring).

2. **Matching Process**: Develop a process for matching mentors with mentees based on goals, skills, and personalities.

3. **Training and Resources**: Train mentors and mentees to set expectations and develop necessary skills.

4. Foster a Supportive Environment

1. **Open Communication**: Encourage open and honest communication between mentors and mentees.

2. **Psychological Safety**: Create a safe space for mentees to share challenges and seek advice without fear of judgment.

5. Integration with Onboarding

1. **Onboarding Support**: Pair new employees with mentors to help them acclimate to the organization's culture and processes.

2. **Initial Guidance**: Provide immediate support for new hires, easing their transition and promoting early engagement.

6. Recognition and Incentives

1. **Acknowledgement**: Recognize and celebrate successful mentorship relationships and milestones.

2. **Incentives**: Consider offering incentives for mentors, such as professional development opportunities, awards, or additional compensation.

7. Continuous Feedback and Improvement

1. **Regular Check-Ins**: Schedule regular check-ins to monitor the progress of mentorship relationships and address any issues.

2. **Feedback Mechanism**: Implement a system for collecting participant feedback to refine and improve the program.

8. Measure Impact and Success

1. **KPIs and Metrics**: Define key performance indicators (KPIs) to measure the mentorship program's success (e.g., employee satisfaction, retention rates, performance improvements).

2. **Surveys and Assessments**: Conduct surveys and assessments to gather data on the program's impact.

9. Promote Inclusivity and Diversity

1. **Diverse Pairings**: Ensure the program promotes varied and inclusive mentorship pairings.

2. **Accessibility**: Make the mentorship program accessible to all employees, regardless of their level or department.

10. Leverage Technology

1. **Mentorship Platforms**: Utilize digital platforms to facilitate mentor-mentee matching, communication, and progress tracking.

2. **Virtual Mentoring**: Incorporate virtual mentoring options to accommodate remote or hybrid work environments.

11. Communicate the Value

1. **Internal Marketing**: Regularly communicate the benefits and successes of the mentorship program through internal channels.

2. **Testimonials and Stories**: Share testimonials and success stories from participants to inspire others to get involved.

Example Implementation Plan

Initiation Phase:

- Secure leadership buy-in.
- Define program objectives and goals.
- Form a mentorship program committee.

Design Phase:

- Develop mentorship models and matching processes.
- Create training materials and resources.
- Set up a mentorship platform or system.

Launch Phase:

- Announce the program organization-wide.
- Begin the mentor-mentee matching process.
- Conduct initial training sessions.

Execution Phase:

- Facilitate regular mentor-mentee meetings.
- Provide ongoing support and resources.
- Monitor progress and collect feedback.

Evaluation Phase:

- Assess the program's impact through KPIs and Feedback.

- Recognize and reward successful mentorships.

- Refine the program based on evaluation results.

By systematically implementing these steps, you can establish a thriving culture of mentorship in your workplace that benefits both individuals and the organization.

CONCLUSION

Leadership Development and Continuous Improvement

Leadership development and continuous improvement are critical to fostering a thriving and adaptable organization. Let's delve into each:

Leadership Development:

1. **Identification of Leadership Traits**: Understanding what qualities make a good leader is essential. Empathy, communication skills, decisiveness, and strategic thinking are often valued.

2. **Training and Mentorship Programs**: Leadership training workshops, seminars, and mentorship opportunities can help cultivate employees' leadership skills.

3. **360-Degree Feedback**: Regular feedback from peers, subordinates, and superiors can provide valuable insights into areas for improvement and strengths.

4. **Promoting a Learning Culture**: Encouraging continuous learning and self-improvement within the organization fosters leadership development at all levels.

5. **Leadership Development Plans**: Creating personalized development plans for aspiring leaders can help them focus on specific areas for growth and track their progress over time.

Continuous Improvement:

1. **Kaizen Philosophy**: Embracing the Kaizen philosophy of continuous improvement, which emphasizes making small, incremental changes over time, can lead to significant improvements in processes and outcomes.

2. **Regular Evaluation and Feedback**: Regular evaluations of processes, systems, and performance metrics allow organizations to identify improvement areas and make necessary adjustments.

3. **Cross-functional collaboration**: Encouraging collaboration across different departments and teams can facilitate sharing of best practices and innovative ideas for improvement.

4. **Experimentation and Innovation**: Creating a culture that encourages experimentation and risk-taking fosters innovation and allows for the discovery of new and more efficient ways of doing things.

5. **Data-Driven Decision Making**: Utilizing data and analytics to inform decision-making processes enables organizations to identify trends, patterns, and areas for improvement with greater precision.

In summary, leadership development and continuous improvement are interconnected aspects of organizational growth. By investing in developing leaders and fostering a culture of continuous improvement, organizations can adapt to changing environments, enhance performance, and achieve long-term success.

Importance of Lifelong Learning

Lifelong workplace learning is crucial for individual and organizational success in today's rapidly evolving world. Here's why:

1. **Adaptation to Change**: Industries are constantly evolving due to technological advancements, market shifts, and changes in consumer behavior. Lifelong learning ensures that employees can adapt to these changes, stay relevant, and remain effective.

2.   **Skill Development**: Continuous learning allows employees to acquire and enhance new skills. This not only boosts individual performance but also improves overall team productivity and efficiency.

3.   **Innovation and Creativity**: Learning new concepts, methodologies, and perspectives fosters innovation and creativity within the workplace. Employees encouraged to learn are more likely to develop fresh ideas and solutions to challenges.

4.   **Employee Engagement and Retention**: Offering opportunities for learning and development increases employee engagement and satisfaction. Employees who feel supported in their growth are likelier to stay with the company than seek opportunities elsewhere.

5.   **Competitive Advantage**: Organizations that prioritize lifelong learning gain a competitive edge in the market. They can innovate faster, adapt to change more effectively and attract top talent who value personal and professional development.

6.   **Leadership Development**: Lifelong learning is essential for grooming future leaders within an organization. Continuous development allows individuals to hone their leadership skills and take on more significant responsibilities as they progress in their careers.

7.   **Cultural Development**: Encouraging a learning culture fosters collaboration, knowledge sharing, and a sense of community within the workplace. It creates an environment where employees feel motivated to grow together and support each other's development.

8.   **Futureproofing**: In a world where job roles are evolving and new professions are emerging, lifelong learning is essential for future-proofing both individuals and organizations. It ensures that employees have the skills and knowledge needed to thrive in the jobs of tomorrow.

Overall, lifelong learning in the workplace is not just a nice to have; it's necessary for staying competitive, fostering innovation, and building a thriving organizational culture.

Developing Leadership Competencies

Developing leadership competencies in the workplace involves a combination of personal development, training programs, practical experience, and organizational support. Here's a breakdown of critical steps to cultivate leadership competencies:

1. **Self-awareness**: Encourage leaders to understand their strengths, weaknesses, values, and motivations. Tools like personality assessments, 360-degree feedback, and reflective practices can aid this process.

2. **Communication**: Effective communication is essential for leadership. Provide training on active listening, clear articulation, empathy, and non-verbal communication. Encourage leaders to adapt their communication style to different audiences and situations.

3. **Emotional Intelligence**: Foster emotional intelligence by promoting self-regulation, empathy, and social skills. Offer workshops or coaching sessions on managing emotions, resolving conflicts, and building positive relationships.

4. **Decision Making**: Train leaders in critical thinking, problem-solving, and decision-making techniques. Please encourage them to consider various perspectives, gather relevant information, and evaluate risks before making decisions.

5. **Strategic Thinking**: Develop leaders' ability to think strategically by aligning their actions with organizational goals and anticipating future challenges. Provide exposure to strategic planning processes and opportunities for cross-functional collaboration.

6. **Team Building**: Equip leaders with the skills to build and lead high-performing teams. Offer training on team dynamics, conflict resolution, delegation, and fostering a culture of collaboration and trust.

7. **Change Management**: Given the dynamic nature of the workplace, leaders should be adept at managing change. Provide resources on change management principles, resilience-building techniques, and strategies for overcoming uncertainty.

8. **Coaching and Mentoring**: Encourage leaders to coach and mentor their team members. Offer coaching skills training, provide constructive feedback, and facilitate employee development.

9. **Innovation and Creativity**: Cultivate a culture of innovation by empowering leaders to foster creativity, experimentation, and continuous improvement. Provide tools and resources to spark innovation and recognize and reward innovative efforts.

10. **Ethical Leadership**: Promote ethical behavior and integrity among leaders. Offer training on ethical decision-making, navigating ethical dilemmas, and fostering a culture of accountability and transparency.

11. **Adaptability**: Help leaders develop adaptability by being open to new ideas, embracing change, and continuously learning and growing. Please encourage them to seek feedback, reflect on their experiences, and adapt their approach.

12. **Resilience**: Equip leaders with resilience-building strategies to navigate challenges and setbacks effectively. Offer resources on stress management, work-life balance, and self-care practices.

13. **Networking and Relationship Building**: Encourage leaders to build and maintain a strong network of professional relationships both within and outside the organization. Provide opportunities for networking, mentorship, and community involvement.

14. **Measurement and Feedback**: Establish mechanisms for assessing leadership competencies and providing feedback. Utilize performance evaluations, 360-degree feedback surveys, and regular check-ins to track progress and identify areas for improvement.

By implementing these strategies, organizations can effectively develop leadership competencies and cultivate a pipeline of capable and resilient leaders who can drive success in the workplace.

Sustaining Growth as A Leader

Sustaining growth as a leader in the workplace involves continuous learning, adaptation, and development. Here are some strategies to help you achieve that:

1. **Set Clear Goals**: Clearly define your personal and professional goals. This will give you direction and purpose, guiding your actions and decisions.

2. **Continuous Learning**: Commit to lifelong learning. Stay updated with industry trends, acquire new skills, and seek out opportunities for professional development.

3. **Seek Feedback**: Seek feedback from peers, supervisors, and team members. Constructive feedback helps you identify areas for improvement and grow as a leader.

4. **Embrace Challenges**: View challenges as opportunities for growth rather than obstacles. Embrace them with a positive mindset and use them to develop resilience and problem-solving skills.

5. **Lead by Example**: Be a role model for your team. In everything you do, demonstrate integrity, accountability, and a strong work ethic. Your actions will inspire others to follow suit.

6. **Empower Your Team**: Foster a culture of trust and empowerment within your team. Delegate responsibilities,

encourage autonomy, and provide support when needed. Empowered teams are more innovative and productive.

7. **Adaptability**: Adaptability is crucial for sustained growth in today's fast-paced world. Be open to change, embrace new ideas, and demonstrate flexibility in your approach to leadership.

8. **Build Relationships**: Cultivate strong relationships with your team members, colleagues, and stakeholders. Effective communication, empathy, and collaboration are essential to building trust and fostering a positive work environment.

9. **Celebrate Successes**: Acknowledge and celebrate your team's achievements. Recognizing their efforts boosts morale and motivates them to continue striving for excellence.

10. **Self-Reflection**: Regularly reflect on your leadership style, strengths, and areas for improvement. Identify areas where you can grow and take proactive steps to address them.

By implementing these strategies, you can sustain your growth as a leader in the workplace and continue to inspire and empower those around you.

Skills of Successful Leaders

Successful supervisors possess a combination of leadership, communication, and interpersonal skills. Here are some key traits they often exhibit:

1. **Clear Communication**: They can articulate goals, expectations, and feedback clearly and effectively to their team members.

2. **Empathy**: They understand their team members' perspectives, needs, and concerns, fostering a supportive and inclusive work environment.

3. **Adaptability**: They can navigate and lead through change, whether it's organizational restructuring, new projects, or shifts in team dynamics.

4. **Problem-solving Skills**: They're adept at identifying issues, analyzing situations, and implementing solutions to overcome challenges.

5. **Decisiveness**: They can make timely and well-informed decisions, even in ambiguous or high-pressure situations.

6. **Delegation**: They know how to delegate tasks effectively, balancing workload distribution while empowering team members to grow and develop their skills.

7. **Accountability**: They hold themselves and their team members accountable for their actions and outcomes, fostering a culture of responsibility and ownership.

8. **Positive Attitude**: They maintain a constructive and optimistic outlook, even in the face of setbacks or obstacles, inspiring motivation and resilience in their team.

9. **Conflict Resolution Skills**: They can address conflicts and disagreements constructively, promoting collaboration and maintaining harmony within the team.

10. **Continual Learning**: They are committed to their professional development and encourage learning and growth among their team members.

11. **Trustworthiness**: They build trust through honesty, integrity, and consistency in their actions and decisions.

12. **Visionary Leadership**: They have a clear vision for the team's goals and direction, inspiring others to work towards a common purpose.

By embodying these traits, successful supervisors can effectively lead their teams to achieve their objectives while fostering a positive and productive work environment.

The Best-Kept Secrets of Successful Supervisors

The best-kept secret of successful supervisors isn't some magical formula or elusive skill; it's effective communication. Successful supervisors excel in communicating openly and empathetically with their team members. Here's why:

1. **Clear Expectations**: They articulate expectations clearly, ensuring everyone understands their roles, responsibilities, and goals. This clarity fosters accountability and minimizes misunderstandings.

2. **Active Listening**: Successful supervisors actively listen to their team members, valuing their input and concerns. Attentively listening builds trust and rapport, creating an environment where employees feel heard and valued.

3. **Constructive Feedback**: They provide regular, constructive feedback that focuses on strengths and areas for improvement. This feedback is specific, actionable, and delivered in a supportive manner, encouraging growth and development.

4. **Empathy**: Successful supervisors understand their team members' perspectives and emotions. They empathize with their struggles, celebrate successes, and offer support during challenging times, fostering a positive and supportive work culture.

5. **Transparency**: They are transparent about the organization's decisions, processes, and changes. Transparency builds trust and credibility, empowering employees to feel informed and engaged.

6. **Adaptability**: Successful supervisors adapt their communication style to the needs of individual team members and

situations. They recognize that effective communication isn't one-size-fits-all and tailor their approach accordingly.

7. **Conflict Resolution**: They address conflicts promptly and constructively, facilitating open dialogue and finding mutually beneficial solutions. Proactive conflict management prevents issues from escalating and maintains a harmonious work environment.

8. **Continuous Improvement**: Successful supervisors are committed to continually improving their communication skills. They seek feedback, reflect on their interactions, and actively work to enhance their communication effectiveness over time.

Effective communication is the cornerstone of successful supervision. It builds trust, fosters collaboration, and drives performance, ultimately leading to tremendous success for supervisors and their teams.

Scenario:

You are the CEO of a mid-sized tech company specializing in developing innovative software solutions for businesses. Your company, Tec Innovate, has been growing steadily over the past five years, but you've recently encountered several significant challenges:

1. Increased Competition: Several new competitors have entered the market, offering similar products at lower prices.

2. Customer Retention: While you have a good customer base, retaining these customers has become difficult due to aggressive marketing and better pricing from competitors.

3. Innovation Stagnation: Your R&D team has hit a roadblock and has yet to release any significant new features or products in the last year.

4. Talent Acquisition: Attracting and retaining top talent has become a struggle due to the competitive job market and lucrative offers from larger tech firms.

5. Economic Uncertainty: The economic climate is uncertain, and concerns about a potential recession could affect your customers' spending on new software solutions.

Exercise:

1. **Define the Problem**: Clearly define the key problems your company is facing.

2. **Analyze the Situation**: Assess the internal and external factors contributing to these problems. This includes a SWOT analysis (Strengths, Weaknesses, Opportunities, Threats).

3. **Develop Strategic Options**: Brainstorm and outline at least three strategic options or initiatives to address these challenges.

4. **Evaluate the Options**: Assess each option's pros and cons. Consider factors such as feasibility, cost, time, and potential impact.

5. **Recommend a Strategy**: Based on your evaluation, recommend one or a combination of strategies to implement. Explain your rationale.

6. **Implementation Plan**: Outline a high-level implementation plan for the chosen strategy. Include key steps, resources required, and a timeline.

7. **Measure Success**: Identify key metrics and milestones to measure the success of your strategy. How will you know if your plan is working?

Example Response:

1. **Define the Problem:**

- Increased competition and price pressure

- Difficulty in retaining customers
- Innovation stagnation
- Challenges in Talent Acquisition and retention
- Economic uncertainty

2. Analyze the Situation:

SWOT Analysis:

Strengths:
- Strong brand reputation
- Loyal customer base
- Experienced leadership team

Weaknesses:
- Slower innovation pipeline
- Limited resources compared to larger competitors

Opportunities:
- Expanding into new markets
- Forming strategic partnerships
- Investing in emerging technologies

Threats:
- Aggressive competition
- Economic downturn
- Talent poaching by larger firms.

3. Develop Strategic Options:

Option 1: Invest in R&D to accelerate innovation and release new products. **Option 2**: Enhance customer retention programs and offer loyalty incentives. **Option 3:** Form strategic partnerships or consider mergers/acquisitions to expand capabilities and market reach.

4. **Evaluate the Options**:

Option 1 Pros**:**

- Revitalizes product offerings.
- Strengthens market position.
- Attracts top talent.

Option 1 Cons:

- High cost
- Long time to market

Option 2 Pros:

- Improves customer loyalty.
- Immediate impact on retention rates.
- Lower cost

Option 2 Cons:

- It does not address innovation directly
- It may not attract new customers

Option 3 Pros:

- Expands capabilities and resources
- Enhances competitive position

Option 3 Cons:

- Complex integration process
- Potential cultural clashes

5. Recommend a Strategy:

- Combine Options 1 and 2: Invest in R&D while enhancing customer retention programs. This dual approach addresses both innovation and customer loyalty.

6. Implementation Plan:

- Phase 1 (0-3 months): Launch loyalty programs and personalized services to boost customer retention.

- Phase 2 (3-12 months): Increase R&D budget, hire additional talent, and initiate new product development projects.

- Phase 3 (12-24 months): Launch new products, assess market response, and refine retention programs based on customer feedback.

7. Measure success:

- Customer retention rates

- Number of new product launches

- Market share growth

- Employee satisfaction and retention rates

- Revenue growth and profitability

Coming Soon!

To continue enhancing your leadership journey, we offer a new book, ***Why Supervisors, Managers, and Leaders Fail.*** This book will help you identify and avoid leaders' pitfalls so you can continue to champion your Leadership style in the workplace.

Check our website for Preorder availability:
broadwaypublishingco.com.

THE FINAL WORD

As we draw this book to a close, let's reflect on our journey together. Through this book, we have explored the multifaceted nature of leadership and delved into the skills necessary for effective leadership in today's workplace. This journey has been about acquiring knowledge and understanding the profound impact of leadership on individuals, teams, and organizations.

The Essence of Leadership

Leadership, at its core, is about influence and inspiration. It is about guiding others towards a shared vision and fostering an environment where everyone feels valued and empowered to contribute their best. The essence of leadership is not confined to a position or title; it is a practice that anyone can adopt regardless of their role within an organization.

We began by exploring the foundational qualities of a leader, including integrity, empathy, and vision. These qualities are the bedrock upon which all other leadership skills are built. Without integrity, a leader cannot be trusted; without empathy, a leader cannot connect; without vision, a leader cannot inspire. While intrinsic to some, these qualities can be cultivated through self-awareness and intentional practice.

Key Leadership Skills Revisited

Throughout this book, we have covered many essential skills for effective leadership. Let us revisit some of the key takeaways:

Communication

Effective communication is the cornerstone of leadership. It involves conveying ideas clearly and persuasively and listening actively and empathetically. As we discussed, leaders must be adept at various forms of communication—verbal, non-verbal, and written. They must also be able to tailor their communication style to suit different audiences and contexts.

Decision-Making

Decision-making is a critical skill that can significantly impact an organization's direction and success. Leaders are often faced with complex and high-stakes decisions. The ability to analyze information, consider different perspectives, and make sound judgments is crucial. We also emphasized the importance of decisiveness and the courage to take responsibility for decisions.

Emotional Intelligence

Emotional intelligence (EI) is the ability to understand and manage one's own emotions and the emotions of others. High EI enables leaders to build stronger relationships, manage stress, and navigate the social complexities of the workplace. We highlighted the components of EI—self-awareness, self-regulation, motivation, empathy, and social skills—and discussed how leaders can enhance these attributes.

Adaptability

In today's rapidly changing work environment, adaptability is a vital skill. Leaders must be open to new ideas, willing to change course when necessary and encourage innovation within their teams. Adaptable leaders can better handle uncertainties and are more likely to lead their organizations to success in a dynamic landscape.

Conflict Resolution

Conflict is an inevitable part of any workplace. Effective leaders do not shy away from conflict but rather address it constructively. We explored various strategies for conflict resolution, including active listening, mediating between parties, and fostering a culture of open communication and respect.

Leadership in Practice

Theory alone is insufficient to develop leadership skills; practical application is key. Throughout the book, we provide numerous examples, case studies, and exercises to help you apply what you have learned. Whether you lead a project, mentor a colleague, or participate in leadership training programs, the opportunities to practice leadership are abundant.

One of the most powerful ways to develop as a leader is through reflection. Regularly reflecting on your experiences, decisions, and interactions can provide valuable insights and promote continuous improvement. Keep a leadership journal, seek feedback from others, and be mindful of your growth journey.

The Future of Leadership

As we look to the future, the leadership landscape will continue to evolve. Technological advancements, demographic shifts, and global interconnectedness are just a few of the factors that will shape the workplace of the future. Leaders of tomorrow will need to be even more agile, culturally aware, and technologically savvy.

One emerging trend is the increasing emphasis on inclusive leadership. Inclusive leaders recognize the value of diversity and strive to create environments where everyone feels they belong. This involves not only diversity in terms of gender, race, and ethnicity but also diversity of thought, experience, and perspective.

Another trend is the growing importance of sustainability and social responsibility. Leaders are now expected to consider the broader impact of their decisions on society and the environment. This shift requires rethinking traditional business models and a commitment to ethical practices.

Your Leadership Journey

As you conclude this book, remember that leadership is a journey, not a destination. It is a continuous process of learning, growing, and adapting. The skills and insights you have gained here are just the beginning. Embrace the challenges and opportunities that come your way, and never stop striving to be a better leader.

Embodying practical leadership principles can significantly impact your organization and the people around you. You can inspire others, drive positive change, and achieve remarkable outcomes.

In closing, I encourage you to stay curious, remain open to new experiences, and keep pushing the boundaries of your leadership capabilities. The workplace of today and tomorrow needs leaders like you—committed, compassionate, and courageous.

Thank you for embarking on this journey with me. Here's to your continued growth and success as a leader. Remember, the leadership journey is lifelong, and the knowledge you've gained here is a stepping stone towards your future endeavors—best of luck.